Plain English

Second Edition

DIANÉ COLLINSON, GILLIAN KIRKUP,
ROBIN KYD AND LYNNE SLOCOMBE

Open University Press
Buckingham and Philadelphia

Open University Press
Celtic Court
22 Ballmoor
Buckingham MK18 1XW

First published in this edition 1992

Written by Diané Collinson, Gillian Kirkup, Robin Kyd and
Lynne Slocombe

A catalogue record of this book is available from the British Library

Library of Congress Cataloging-in-Publication Data

Plain English/edited by Diané Collinson: [written by Diané
    Collinson . . . et al.]. – 2nd ed.
        p.   cm.
    Includes bibliographical references.
    ISBN 0–335–15675–4 (pbk.)
    1. English language – Rhetoric.   2. English language –
Grammar – 1950–   I. Collinson, Diané, 1930–   .
PE1408.P543   1992
808'.042 – dc20   91–46607
                                                                          CIP

Typeset by Type Study, Scarborough
Printed and bound in Great Britain by
Billings Limited, Worcester

Contents

Introduction

Plain English developed out of an idea that began in the Open University's South West region. There, some years ago, five part-time arts-faculty tutors joined with me to produce a set of workbooks for students who had been out of touch with formal education for some time and who wanted to revise or develop some basic writing abilities. Those workbooks were known as *Open Daily*.

Soon after, I was invited by the Open University's technology faculty to collaborate with three of its members, Gillian Kirkup, Robin Kyd and Lynne Slocombe, in producing an adaptation of *Open Daily* for their T101 Foundation Course students. The result was the first edition of *Plain English*.

This new edition of *Plain English* has been prepared to meet the needs of all students who wish to improve their writing skills. Like its predecessor, it opens with an introductory quiz. The quiz is followed by sections on punctuation, spelling, grammar, style, and references and bibliographies. Each section deals step by step with basic difficulties and provides exercises to help you test your understanding. Answers are provided for all the exercises. The whole programme of work has been designed not to encroach too much on your routine study time. The exercises are arranged in groups, and you should find it possible to work through a group over a cup of coffee or on a bus or train journey.

The introductory quiz should help you in two ways. First, it will give you a broad idea of the subject matter covered in *Plain English*. Second, it should help you to decide which sections will be of most use to you. You may find that your family and friends may enjoy doing the quiz and talking about it. Note that the answers to the quiz follow immediately after it.

There are three things I should like to suggest:

1 Please try to work all the way through any section you choose to tackle, restraining yourself from looking at answers until you have made a thorough attempt to complete an exercise.
2 Do develop the habit of keeping your dictionary by you, using it when recommended to, and looking up words whenever you are in doubt as to meanings and spellings. There are also 'spell checks'

available on word processor packages but please remember that they do not include definitions of words or their uses in various contexts.

3 Be alert to everything you read, from advertisements to textbooks, to see if it is clear, accurate and concise in a way that is appropriate to it. This will help you to develop your critical abilities. Remember that clear writing means clear thinking.

I hope that you find *Plain English* enjoyable and helpful.

For her very careful typing of the drafts of this revision of *Plain English*, and for her lively interest in the whole project, I would like to thank Maggie Ovenden.

Diané Collinson

1 Introductory quiz

This quiz consists of thirty-eight examples of incorrect, sloppy or thoughtless English.

For each example, please do three things:

1 Spot the fault and encircle it.
2 *Briefly* describe what is wrong.
3 Wherever possible, write a correct or improved version.

Note Describing exactly what is wrong can be difficult. You are not expected to give full technical descriptions of grammatical and other errors. It will be quite enough to say such things as 'grammar wrong', 'meaning confused', 'punctuation wrong', 'spelling wrong' and so on. Most of the examples present outright errors for you to spot and correct, but a few are instances of bad style (cliché, jargon, wordiness, etc.) and you may feel it not worth while trying to rewrite one or two of these examples.

1 I have now discussed the proposal for restocking all 500 freezers with my colleagues.

Fault

Correction

2 He was definately on the wrong side of the law.

Fault

Correction

3 Today pneumatic tyres are fitted to practically all road vehicles, originally they were developed for use on bicycles.

Fault

Correction

4 When the heyday of science-fiction and horror films is over.

Fault

Correction

5 The development of breeder reactors completely change the economics of ore extraction and boost the known reserves of nuclear energy very considerably.

Fault

Correction

6 Neither knowledge nor skill are needed.

Fault

Correction

7 The project, having been approved, the firm began to recruit the necessary staff.

Fault

Correction

8   There were less visitors than usual.

Fault

Correction

9   The seminar ended by an open discussion.

Fault

Correction

10 The decision to computerize the accounting system has badly effected our relations with our customers.

Fault

Correction

11 The driver of a car, which does not comply with these regulations, is liable to a fine or imprisonment.

Fault

Correction

12 Many birds are protected by law nowadays, i.e. the osprey, the golden eagle, the buzzard and the bittern.

Fault

Correction

13 Manufacturors of toys have a responsibility to make them safe.

Fault

Correction

14 The remuneration received by the subordinate officials of this organization exceeds by a very considerable proportion what is generally placed on offer by other comparable firms.

Fault

Correction

15 This drug has proved successful in a percentage of cases.

Fault

Correction

16 Organizational structure must provide for the coordination of functions and activities in order that interdependent members of the organization and subunits interact in harmony with each other and with other sectors and activities of society in the achievement of the organization's goals and objectives and the delivery of the services it provides.

Fault

Correction

17 The vehicle has it's own reserve power supply.

Fault

Correction

18 His condition can only be alleviated by drugs.

Fault

Correction

19 After adding carefully a few drops of anti-foam oil, the bubbles
disappear.

Fault

Correction

20 Their five-year mission was to boldly go where no one had gone
before.

Fault

Correction

21 We immediately contacted anyone whom we suspected had received a faulty vehicle.

Fault

Correction

22 It is necessary to forecast the number, duration and geographical
distribution of telephone calls, usually referred to as the telephone
traffic in six or seven years' time.

Fault

Correction

23 In this day and age, while industry is grinding to a halt, one can feel
the wind of change heralding the arrival of a new climate of opinion.

Fault

Correction

24 I have outlined below the reasons that have led to them being given appointments in these departments.

Fault

Correction

25 The new parameters for the jobs of the employees were fully described to them by the director.

Fault

Correction

26 Data that is more than five years old is of limited use.

Fault

Correction

27 The houses erected should be broken down into types.

Fault

Correction

28 The corporation has not asked for any advice and I do not doubt its ability to deal with the immediate situation themselves.

Fault

Correction

29 He has been more successful than me.

Fault

Correction

30 I practiced at the terminal for several hours each week.

Fault

Correction

31 How will a driver – of a furniture van – on a motorway – perform in a strong – gusting side-wind?

Fault

Correction

32 The minister agreed in principle to a new urban public transport system development plan.

Fault

Correction

33 There were yellow lines down all the streets and the car parks were full, so I couldn't find nowhere to park the car.

Fault

Correction

34 The cause of the delay in laying the foundations was due to exceptionally heavy rain flooding the area.

Fault

Correction

35 One short inspection was not enough to assertain the extent of the damage.

Fault

Correction

36 It was certainly him, and not the owner of the car, who now came running along the drive.

Fault

Correction

37 When the scheme is finished, all local roads will connect up with the main relief road.

Fault

Correction

38 Dr Robert Marshall and Dr Maria Marshall recently announced their new treatment; our picture shows Dr Robert Marshall and his wife, Maria, arriving at the press conference.

Fault

Correction

Answers to introductory quiz

1 I have now discussed the proposal for restocking all 500 freezers (with my colleagues.)

    Fault   Grammar: wrong position of words.
    Correction   I have now discussed with my colleagues the proposal for restocking all 500 freezers.

2 He was (definately) on the wrong side of the law.

    Fault   Spelling
    Correction   He was definitely on the wrong side of the law.

3 Today pneumatic tyres are fitted to practically all road ve-hicles (,) originally they were developed for use on bicycles.

    Fault   Punctuation: comma inadequate.
    Correction   Today pneumatic tyres are fitted to practically all road vehicles; originally they were developed for use on bicycles.

4 (When the heyday of science-fiction and horror films is over.)

    Fault   Grammar: not a sentence.
    Correction   (e.g.) I shall be glad when the heyday of science-fiction and horror films is over.

5 The development of breeder reactors completely (change) the economics of ore extraction and (boost) the known reserves of nuclear energy very considerably.

    Fault   Grammar.
    Correction   The development of breeder reactors completely changes the economics of ore extraction and boosts the known reserves of nuclear energy very considerably.

6　Neither knowledge nor skill ⟨are⟩ needed.

Fault　Grammar.
Correction　Neither knowledge nor skill is needed.

7　The project ⟨,⟩ having been approved, the firm began to recruit
the necessary staff.

Fault　Punctuation: wrongly inserted comma.
Correction　The project having been approved, the firm began to
recruit the necessary staff.

8　There were ⟨less⟩ visitors than usual.

Fault　Grammar: wrong use of *less*.
Correction　There were fewer visitors than usual.

9　The seminar ended ⟨by⟩ an open discussion.

Fault　Grammar: wrong word used.
Correction　The seminar ended with an open discussion.

10　The decision to computerize the accounting system has badly
⟨effected⟩ our relations with our customers.

Fault　Grammar: confusion of *affect* and *effect*.
Correction　The decision to computerize the accounting system
has badly affected our relations with our customers.

11　The driver of a car ⟨,⟩ which does not comply with these
regulations ⟨,⟩ is liable to a fine or imprisonment.

Fault　Punctuation: wrongly inserted commas.
Correction　The driver of a car which does not comply with these
regulations is liable to a fine or imprisonment.

12　Many birds are protected by law nowadays, ⟨i.e.⟩ the osprey,
the golden eagle, the buzzard and the bittern.

Fault　Style: incorrect use of i.e. (that is).
Correction　Many birds are protected by law nowadays, e.g. [for
example] the osprey, the golden eagle, the buzzard and the
bittern.

13 (Manufacturors) of toys have a responsibility to make them safe.

Fault Spelling.
Correction Manufacturers of toys have a responsibility to make them safe.

14 The remuneration received by the subordinate officials of this organization exceeds by a very considerable proportion what is generally placed on offer by other comparable firms.

Fault Style: pompous and jargonistic.
Correction Compared with similar firms, this one pays its junior employees a lot.

15 This drug has proved successful in a (percentage) of cases.

Fault Style: meaningless use of *percentage*.
Correction This drug has proved successful in a large [small?] proportion of cases.

16 Organizational structure must provide for the coordination of functions and activities in order that interdependent members of the organization and subunits interact in harmony with each other and with other sectors and activities of society in the achievement of the organization's goals and objectives and the delivery of the services it provides.

Fault Style: jargon.
Correction The organization must have a structure that enables all its members to work together to achieve its aims.

17 The vehicle has (it's) own reserve power supply.

Fault Punctuation: wrong use of apostrophe.
Correction The vehicle has its own reserve power supply.

18 His condition can (only) be alleviated by drugs.

Fault Grammar: ambiguous placing of *only*.
Correction Only drugs can alleviate his condition.
Or Drugs can only alleviate [but not cure] his condition.

19 (After adding) carefully a few drops of anti-foam oil, the bubbles disappear.

Fault Grammar.
Correction After a few drops of anti-foam oil have been carefully added, the bubbles disappear.

20 Their five-year mission was (to boldly go) where no one had gone before.

Fault Grammar: split infinitive.
Correction Their five-year mission was to go boldly where no one had gone before.

21 We immediately contacted anyone (whom) we suspected had received a faulty vehicle.

Fault Grammar: *whom* for *who*.
Correction We immediately contacted anyone who we suspected had received a faulty vehicle.

22 It is necessary to forecast the number, duration and geographical distribution of telephone calls, usually referred to as the telephone traffic ◯ in six or seven years' time.

Fault Punctuation: comma missing.
Correction It is necessary to forecast the number, duration and geographical distribution of telephone calls, usually referred to as the telephone traffic, in six or seven years' time.

23 In this day and age, while industry is grinding to a halt, one can feel the wind of change heralding the arrival of a new climate of opinion.

Fault Style: clichés throughout.
Correction Industry is not thriving nowadays but one senses that new ideas are on their way.

24　I have outlined below the reasons that have led to ⟨them⟩ being given appointments in these departments.

Fault　Grammar.
Correction　I have outlined below the reasons which have led to their being given appointments in these departments.

25　The new ⟨parameters⟩ for the jobs of the employees were fully described to them by the director.

Fault　Style: incorrect use of technical (mathematical) term.
Correction　The employees were given full descriptions of their new jobs by the director.

26　Data that ⟨is⟩ more than five years old ⟨is⟩ of limited use.

Fault　Grammar.
Correction　Data that are more than five years old are of limited use.

27　The houses erected should be ⟨broken down⟩ into types.

Fault　Style: ludicrous effect of metaphor.
Correction　The houses erected should be classified according to type.

28　The corporation ⟨has⟩ not asked for any advice and I do not doubt ⟨its⟩ ability to deal with the immediate situation ⟨themselves.⟩

Fault　Grammar.
Correction　The corporation has not asked for any advice and I do not doubt its ability to deal with the immediate situation itself.
Or　The corporation have not asked for any advice and I do not doubt their ability to deal with the immediate situation themselves.

29　He has been more successful than ⟨me.⟩

Fault　Grammar.
Correction　He has been more successful than I [have].

30 I (practiced) at the terminal for several hours each week.

Fault Spelling.
Correction I practised at the terminal for several hours each week.

31 How will a driver ⊖ of a furniture van ⊖ on a motorway ⊖ perform in a strong ⊖ gusting side-wind?

Fault Punctuation: unnecessary dashes.
Correction How will a driver of a furniture van on a motorway perform in a strong gusting side-wind?

32 The minister agreed in principle to a new urban public transport system development plan.

Fault Style: bad use of nouns as adjectives.
Correction The minister agreed in principle to a new plan for developing a system of public transport in the city.

33 There were yellow lines down all the streets and the car parks were full, so I (couldn't find nowhere) to park the car.

Fault Grammar: double negative.
Correction There were yellow lines down all the streets and the car parks were full, so I couldn't find anywhere to park the car.
Or . . . so I could find nowhere to park the car.

34 The (cause) of the delay in laying the foundations (was due) to exceptionally heavy rain flooding the area.

Fault Style: redundancy.
Correction The cause of the delay in laying the foundations was the exceptionally heavy rain flooding the area.
Or The delay in laying the foundations was due to exceptionally heavy rain flooding the area.

35 One short inspection was not enough to (assertain) the extent of the damage.

Fault Spelling.
Correction One short inspection was not enough to ascertain the extent of the damage.

36 It was certainly (him) , and not the owner of the car, who now came running along the drive.

Fault Grammar.
Correction It was certainly he, and not the owner of the car, who now came running along the drive.

37 When the scheme is finished, all local roads will connect (up) with the main relief road.

Fault Grammar: redundant word.
Correction When the scheme is finished, all local roads will connect with the main relief road.

38 Dr Robert Marshall and Dr Maria Marshall recently announced their new treatment; our picture shows Dr Robert Marshall and his wife, Maria, arriving at the press conference.

Fault Sexist language.
Correction Dr Robert Marshall and Dr Maria Marshall recently announced their new treatment; our picture shows them (or, the husband-wife team/wife-husband team, depending on their positions in the picture) arriving at the press conference.

2 Punctuation

Full stops and capital letters

The full stop is used to mark the end of all sentences except direct questions (?) and exclamations (!).

A capital letter is used to mark the beginnings of all sentences.

Exercise 1

The passage below contains five sentences. Supply capital letters and full stops where necessary. No other punctuation is needed.

Brunel's critics still refused to be convinced and now maintained that when the time came to remove the centering altogether the bridge would surely collapse the engineer himself had no doubts whatever about his bridge but he ruled that the centres should not be removed finally until it had stood through another winter the suspicion that this was due not so much to excessive caution as to an impish sense of humour is hard to resist certainly the fact that the bridge was standing entirely free for nine months while his jealous opponents supposed that the centering was still helping to support it was a joke that Brunel must have relished keenly its point was revealed and his critics confounded by a violent storm one autumn night in 1839 which blew all the useless centering down

---

A full stop is also used with initials and abbreviations. For example:

I. K. Brunel, e.g., ed. (editor), p. (page), ch. (chapter), no. (number), vol. (volume), a.m., p.m., co., e.m.f. (electromotive force), etc.

You may be puzzled by practices relating to the omission of full stops with contractions and capital initials. It is now quite common and acceptable to omit full stops from capital initials such as BBC, UK, OU, VHF, DDT, TV, but it is still perfectly acceptable to use full stops if you prefer. Full stops are now commonly omitted from contractions (i.e. shortenings of words that keep the final letter of the whole word) such as Dr, Mrs, 3rd edn (third edition). Again, if you think this is an unnecessary distinction, it is entirely acceptable to write contractions with full stops.

Exercise 2

Add full stops to these sentences:

(a) Mr and Mrs J B Jones, who live at 23 St James's Gardens, told P C Alderbank that they had been woken at 3 a m by the sound of glass breaking and had seen a man running out of the house opposite, no 26

(b) The T V programme I liked so much was on either BBC 1 or BBC 2 and was presented by a Dr T W Fox

(c) In March 1979 the Royal Society held a discussion meeting on nuclear magnetic resonance (nmr) of intact biological systems organized by Prof R J P Williams, FRS, Prof E R Andrew and Dr G K Radda

---

It is incorrect to add a full stop to the *symbols* for units of measurement and chemical elements. Here are some examples:

m	metre	C	carbon
kg	kilogram	Fe	iron
V	volt	U	uranium

A capital letter is used to mark the beginning of each sentence. If you can, avoid opening a sentence with symbols and numbers, which should be spelled out if used.

Capitals are used for the first letters of the names of people, places, months, days of the week, etc. They are also used for the first letters of all the main words in the titles of organizations, people, books, periodicals or journals, newspapers, etc. Here are a few examples:

the Open University, the Bishop of Oxford, *Animal Farm*, *Journal of Materials Science*, the *Independent*.

The old rule of using a capital letter for the particular and a small letter for the general is still a helpful guide. For example:

Heathrow Airport is one of the world's busiest international airports.

The figures in this book are excellent; Figure 14, for example, shows all the complexity of a modern telecommunication network without being cluttered with unnecessary detail.

It is important to be consistent throughout your writing.

Exercise 3

Mark the letters in this passage that are incorrectly or inconsistently capitalized. Add capitals where necessary.

within the wider community of british universities the Open University is the only one which as a general rule demands no Entrance Qualifications of its Students. this means that Foundation courses play a vital role in its teaching system. They form the bridge between students of enormously varied Educational backgrounds and the Higher-level Courses that will enable them to become Graduates.

Beware one or two traps when writing about technical subjects. I shall deal with these in what follows.

Do not be misled into thinking that, because a recognized set of initials is in capitals, the term itself takes capitals. Here are some examples:

AM	amplitude modulation
PVC	polyvinyl chloride
RAM	random-access memory
TNT	trinitrotoluene
UHF	ultra-high frequency

The best example to keep in mind is

TV	television

Capitals are *not* used for the first letters of the names of units of measurement or of chemical elements and compounds. You will know at least some of the names of units of measurement used by technologists:

second, kilogram, volt, watt, ampere, metre.

The point to note here is that none of them has a capital first letter, even though many of them are taken from personal names. The watt, for example, is named after James Watt (1736–1819).

Even if you are not at all sure what a chemical element is, you are familiar with the names of several:

iron, aluminium, iodine, tin, neon, arsenic, oxygen, copper, hydrogen, uranium, plutonium, silver, gold.

You are probably familiar with the names of at least a few chemical compounds. For example:

carbon dioxide, sulphuric acid, butane, sodium chloride.

None of them requires a capital letter.

Exercise 4

Add *capitals* and full stops to this passage, which contains six sentences. All other punctuation is supplied.

the castner cell underwent various slight modifications during the first quarter of the century, but in 1924 the american j c downs patented a cell for the production of sodium from fused sodium chloride this consisted of a steel tank lined with firebrick containing a massive cylindrical graphite anode projecting through the base, surrounded coaxially by a cathode of iron gauze by adding calcium chloride to the sodium chloride, the melting-point of the electrolyte is reduced from 800 °C to 505 °C the energy efficiency of the downs cell process from salt to sodium is about three times greater than that of the composite process of first producing sodium hydroxide in a mercury cell, followed by further electrolysis in a castner cell however, both processes were in operation in 1950 the price of sodium in the usa dropped from $2.00 per pound in 1890 to $0.15 per pound in 1946

The comma

There are simple, definite rules about the use of the full stop at the end of sentences. There are no equally simple rules for all the various uses of the comma. Putting a comma in, or leaving one out, at a particular place in a sentence is not just a matter of right or wrong punctuation. The comma may give part of the sentence a different emphasis, or it may change the meaning of the sentence, so the decision on how to use the comma will depend on what you want to say.

There is scope for personal preferences in the use of the comma: one writer will put one in where another will leave it out. It has been remarked that:

The correct use of the comma – if there is such a thing as 'correct' use – can only be acquired by common sense, observation and taste.

E. Gowers, *The Complete Plain Words*, 3rd edn
(Penguin, 1987), p. 156

One use of the comma is to separate items in a list:

The engine, the gearbox, the clutch and the brakes had all been repaired.

Or

The engine, the gearbox, the clutch, and the brakes had all been repaired.

In this sentence the comma before *and* is optional. Generally speaking, no comma is placed before *and*, but in some lists a comma before the final *and* may be needed to avoid ambiguity:

Shops that will be opening in the centre include branches of Boots, W. H. Smith, Jones and Jones, and Woolworths.

Exercise 5

Put commas in the following sentences:

(a) Your home may be heated by solid fuel oil gas or electricity.

(b) Resources are defined as energy materials labour and capital.

(c) He found he needed several metres of electric cable three junction boxes a packet of insulated staples four light-switches and an assortment of tools.

Commas are also used to separate descriptive words when several are used together:

Glass is a hard, brittle, transparent material.

Dinneford's Gripe Mixture quickly, gently brings up wind.

Notice that commas are not required in this next example:

This important new discovery was reported in a recent scientific paper.

Can you see why commas are used in the first two examples, but not in that last one? In the next two sentences the difference should be clearer:

The new experimental procedures are intended to improve safety in the laboratory.

This new, experimental traffic scheme will operate for one month initially.

In the first sentence 'new experimental procedures' implies that there were old experimental procedures, but in the second sentence the suggestion is that the old traffic scheme was not experimental. Without the comma, 'new' describes 'experimental procedures'; with the comma, 'new' describes only the 'traffic scheme'. Another way of looking at it is this: when descriptive words are separated by commas, they each act *independently* on the word they are describing.

Exercise 6

Add commas where appropriate:

(a) Copper is a malleable ductile metal.

(b) Many new electronic gadgets have appeared in recent years.

(c) The new crystals tended to be long smooth whip-like filaments.

Another use of commas is to separate a sequence of closely related clauses:

Oxygen and nitrogen are gases, nearly all the metallic elements are solids, but of all the chemical elements only bromine and mercury are liquids at room temperature.

Put the peeled potatoes into a pan, cover them with cold water, add a pinch of salt and boil for 15–20 minutes.

Water evaporates from the oceans, forms clouds in the atmosphere, falls as rain, drains from the land as surface water into the rivers, and flows back into the oceans.

A clause, by the way, is simply a part of a sentence that has a verb in it, and a verb is a 'doing' or 'being' word such as *are*, *put*, *boil*, *evaporates*, *flows* in the above examples.

Sometimes a sentence has just two clauses joined by a word such as *but*, *or*, or *and*:

Swan's first carbon-filament lamp was made in 1848, but its life was too brief to be useful.

Shortly afterwards Francis Hauksbee demonstrated that charged bodies repel as well as attract each other, and in 1729 Stephen Gray made the very important contribution of distinguishing between conductors (mainly metals) and non-conductors.

T. K. Derry and T. I. Williams, *A Short History of Technology*, paperback edn (Oxford University Press, 1970), pp. 608–9

21

The commas in those two examples are not absolutely essential, but they do ease the task of reading them. Thus, as a rule, a comma is put before *but* or *or* joining two clauses. A comma is preferable before an *and* that joins two lengthy clauses (as in the last example), but a comma is not required before the *and* joining two short clauses:

I went to the library and I borrowed a book on astronomy.

When both clauses have the same subject, as here (*I*), the subject is often left out the second time.

I went to the library and borrowed a book on astronomy.

A common misuse of the comma is to separate two main clauses that are not linked by *and*. Here is an example of this misuse:

Cellulose forms the main constituent of plant-cell walls and textile fibres, it is an example of a natural polymer.

The comma is inadequate there. A stronger break is required. The sentence would be better punctuated with a semicolon:

Cellulose forms the main constituent of plant-cell walls and textile fibres; it is an example of a natural polymer.

We will be looking at the semicolon more fully later. For the present, be on your guard against using the comma for a job that it is not strong enough to tackle.

Another common mistake is to place a single comma between a subject and its verb. Here are two examples of this wrong use of a comma:

Many new electronic gadgets, have appeared in recent years.

The construction of the new furnace, was completed ahead of schedule.

The commas in those sentences are not needed.

Exercise 7

Add commas where appropriate to these sentences:

(a)   The engine stalled the brakes failed and the car started to roll backwards.

(b)   Britain now has a system as advanced as any in the world and other countries are adopting similar systems.

(c)   I was finding it hard to keep up with the course and had missed one or two lectures but I made a point of going to all the tutorials and handing in my essays on time.

(d)   Seaside habitats are equally rich and varied and provide great contrasts in species.

Exercise 8 (revision)

Add *commas*, capitals and full stops to these passages:

(a) all matter is made up of atoms and all atoms are made up of an inner nucleus (plural: nuclei) surrounded by electrons almost the whole mass of the atom is concentrated in the nucleus but the nucleus is much smaller than the whole atom the bulk of the nucleus is made up of protons and neutrons all the atoms of a particular chemical element contain the same number of protons and this number is known as the atomic number of the element the atomic number of hydrogen is 1 that of carbon is 6 and that of oxygen is 8 this means that all hydrogen atoms contain 1 proton all carbon atoms contain 6 protons and all oxygen atoms contain 8 protons.

(b) the pressure volume and temperature of a fixed quantity of gas are interrelated boyle's law states that at constant temperature the volume of a given mass of gas is inversely proportional to the pressure and charles's law states that at constant pressure the volume of a given mass of gas is directly proportional to the absolute temperature for a mole of gas these two laws may be combined in the gas equation $pV = RT$ in this equation p is the pressure V is the volume R is the gas constant and T is the absolute temperature gases do not strictly obey the gas laws but follow them more and more closely as the pressure of the gas is reduced.

We will be looking at more uses of the comma on pages 25–7 and 30–33.

The semicolon

Here is some excellent advice. It summarizes all you need to know about the semicolon.

> Do not be afraid of the semicolon; it can be most useful. It marks a longer pause, a more definite break in the sense, than the comma; at the same time it says 'Here is a clause or sentence too closely related to what has gone before to be cut off by a full stop.' The semicolon is a stronger version of the comma.
> *The Complete Plain Words*, p. 173

Exercise 9

In each of the following sentences, pick out the comma that should be replaced by the semicolon:

(a) Heavy chemicals are essentially those produced in bulk and used in large quantities, fine chemicals are made on a comparatively small scale, some indeed in quantities of only a pound or two.

(b) However, technology does not make the only claim on manpower, planning, to be mentioned in a moment, also requires a comparatively high level of specialized talent.

(c) Fox Talbot's sensitive material, like Daguerre's, was silver iodide, formed not more than a day before use as a thin film on paper which was brushed successively with solutions of silver nitrate and potassium iodide, the sensitivity to light was increased by further treatment with gallic acid, the sensitizing properties of this having been discovered in 1837 by J. B. Reade, another British pioneer.

The semicolon is also used as a stronger version of the comma to mark groupings within lists, or to separate phrases that already contain commas. For example:

And all over England towns that are historic today were as yet empty sites: Newcastle, Hull and Liverpool in the north; Boston and Kings Lynn in the east; Portsmouth and Salisbury in the south; Plymouth and Ludlow in the west.

W. G. Hoskins, *The Making of the English Landscape*
(Penguin, 1970), p. 85

Refer to pp. 28–9 if the colon in this sentence puzzles you.

Exercise 10 (revision)

Add *semicolons*, commas, full stops and capitals to this passage.

although this branch of the chemical industry is the one with which the general public most frequently comes into direct contact it is nevertheless one about which many misconceptions exist plastics are often spoken of as though there was little difference between the various kinds in fact they differ enormously in their properties plastics are often thought of as new substances in fact they have been in use for a century plastics are often regarded as cheap substitutes for other and better constructional materials such as wood metal and natural textiles in fact many have found favour on their own merits and often are far from cheap.

The comma (continued)

Commas may be used to mark off a phrase or word added to a sentence that is already grammatically complete. Here are some examples:

The construction of the new furnace, a difficult and costly operation, was completed ahead of schedule.

Mr Brown, a brewery worker from Burton upon Trent, has been an Open University student for three years.

Some of his hearers, however, thought he was joking.

Check that in each example the word or words between the commas could be omitted without making the sentence ungrammatical. For example, if we remove the middle phrase of the first example we get:

The construction of the new furnace was completed ahead of schedule.

We are left with a grammatically complete sentence.

When I say that the sentence is grammatically complete without that phrase, I am not suggesting that its omission does not alter the meaning of the sentence.

Whether or not a word such as 'however' should be separated by commas (or a comma) depends on the way it is being used. The next two examples will show what I mean:

However, hard as this theory is to understand, it will prove most useful once you have learnt it.

25

However hard you try to explain it to me I am sure I shall never understand it.

Exercise 11

Add commas where appropriate:

(a)   The steelworkers' representative a foundryman from Humberside argued for rapid modernization.

(b)   It was his spelling not his punctuation that he needed to improve.

(c)   He had no doubt a speech carefully prepared for the occasion.

(d)   These incidents however trivial in themselves are liable to lead to more serious demonstrations.

Now consider this sentence:

Having obtained planning permission, the company went ahead and built the factory.

The 'root' of this sentence is:

The company went ahead and built the factory.

The subject of this sentence is 'the company'. The phrase 'having obtained planning permission' could equally well have been added after the subject, thus:

The company, having obtained planning permission, went ahead and built the factory.

Both versions of that sentence have the same meaning.
Now look at this sentence:

The company having obtained planning permission, the objectors to the factory felt they had lost their case.

This time the 'root' is:

The objectors to the factory felt they had lost their case.

The subject of the sentence (and of the 'root', of course) is 'the objectors to the factory'. 'The company' in this sentence is not the subject but is a necessary part of the phrase 'the company having obtained planning permission', from which it must not be separated. A wrongly inserted comma would completely confuse the meaning:

The company, having obtained planning permission, the objectors to the factory felt they had lost their case.

Here 'the company' looks as if it is the subject, but when the reader gets to 'the objectors' it becomes evident that the rest of the sentence does not have anything for 'the company' to be the subject of. In this example the comma after 'company' is evidently *wrong*.

Compare these two examples:

The company went ahead and built the factory without having obtained planning permission.

The company went ahead and built the factory, without having obtained planning permission.

Here neither sentence is wrongly punctuated. Can you see what the effect of the comma is? The first sentence is a neutral statement of the facts, but the comma in the second sentence emphasizes 'without having obtained planning permission' and suggests an irregularity in the company's action.

Exercise 12

Add commas where appropriate:

(a) The fire having been lit for some time the room was quite warm.

(b) The fire having been lit for some time needed stoking.

(c) Obtaining planning permission for this factory will not be easy.

(d) The results of his early experiments being positive he was encouraged to embark on a more ambitious programme of research.

(e) The charge on the anode being positive attracts the negatively charged anions.

There is more on the comma on pp. 30–33.

The colon

There is one main use of the colon: to introduce something. It may be a list of items, a statement offered as an explanation, illustration or elaboration of what has gone before, or a quotation. You may have noticed that colons are used frequently in this book, mainly to introduce examples and exercises. Here are a few more colons:

There are four ways in which a nucleus can alter itself: fission, alpha emission, beta emission, and gamma emission.

Henri Becquerel also discovered the most troublesome attribute of radioactivity: its biological effects, actual and potential.

The Times commented: 'The economy has been in trouble for several months.'

A particular instance of this use of the colon is to introduce a series of clauses, sentences, or even paragraphs, each of which begins on a new line, often numbered or lettered. In the first of the examples that follow, the colon introduces three separate sentences (questions); in the second example there is just a single sentence.

1.7   At the outset of the Inquiry I posed three questions which appeared to me to be sufficient to cover all issues which had then been indicated. These questions were:

(1)   Should oxide fuel from United Kingdom reactors be reprocessed in this country at all, whether at Windscale or elsewhere?

(2)   If yes, should such reprocessing be carried on at Windscale?

(3)   If yes, should the reprocessing plant be about double the estimated size to handle United Kingdom oxide fuels and be used, as to the spare capacity, for reprocessing foreign fuels?

The Windscale Inquiry. Report by the Hon. Mr Justice Parker
(HMSO, 1978), pp. 1–2

11.1   Accidents may conveniently be divided into:

(a)   accidents involving a release of radioactivity which does not escape beyond the site boundary and thus does not expose the public;

(b)   accidents which do involve a release beyond the site boundary;

(c)   accidents during transport.

The Windscale Inquiry. Report, p. 64

Notice also the use of semicolons in the last example.

Exercise 14

Add punctuation to the following:

(a)   Four types of malt whisky are made in Scotland Campbeltown Highland Islay and Lowland.

(b)   Time is short sixteen months is all we have.

(c)   Charles Darwin wrote 'I am convinced that Natural Selection has been the main but not exclusive means of modification.'

Exercise 15 (revision)

Add *colons*, commas, full stops and capitals to this passage:

chapman develops three basic scenarios for future patterns of fuel demand in britain 'business-as-usual' 'technical-fix' and 'low-growth' scenarios these represent respectively the virtually unrestrained projection of present trends the introduction of some technical changes to effect a more moderate growth in fuel demand and more radical proposals to effect a very definite restriction in the growth of fuel demand and aimed eventually at stabilizing demand for each case chapman explores how the various components of total fuel demand would change and the policy options that would need to be exercised to supply the various demands this exploration is succinctly conveyed but rests on considerable analysis and chapman's specialist knowledge of energy demands and the fuel industries.

The comma (concluded)

It is not always necessary (and in some cases it is wrong) to separate a subordinate clause from the main part of a sentence, but, if the meaning of the sentence is thereby clarified, commas should be used to mark off the subordinate clause. 'Subordinate' simply means that the clause so named depends on another and cannot stand as a sentence on its own. In the opening sentence of this paragraph, 'if the meaning of the sentence is thereby clarified' is a subordinate clause, and is marked off with commas. On the other hand, 'commas should be used to mark off the subordinate clause' is not a subordinate clause; give it a capital letter and its own full stop and it will stand on its own as a respectable sentence.

Consider the following sentences and notice how they are built up by adding successive subordinate clauses, each separated from the rest of the sentence by a comma or commas:

The social services should receive a larger share of our national wealth.

If the social services are to meet the increasing demands placed on them, they should receive a larger share of our national wealth.

If, as many people have argued, the social services are to meet the increasing demands placed on them, they should receive a larger share of our national wealth.

We must consider motorways as part of a national transport system.

When we assess the need for motorways, we must consider them as part of a national transport system.

When we assess the need for motorways, which are not as important as hospitals, we must consider them as part of a national transport system.

When we assess the need for motorways, which, when judged by these criteria, are not as important as hospitals, we must consider them as part of a national transport system.

It is important to remember that if you mark off a clause in the middle of a sentence, rather than at the beginning or the end, you must use a pair of commas; for a single comma will hide, rather than reveal, the structure of your sentence. Here is an example of such misuse:

Commas, when used to mark off a clause must be used in pairs.

It should, of course, be:

Commas, when used to mark off a clause, must be used in pairs.

Look back at the sentence above that begins, 'It is important . . .' Towards the end of that sentence I inserted 'rather than reveal' into the clause, 'for a single comma will hide the structure of your sentence', thus:

. . . you must use a pair of commas, for a single comma will hide, rather than reveal, the structure of your sentence.

But watch what happens when I am careless and miss out the comma after 'rather than reveal':

. . . you must use a pair of commas, for a single comma will hide, rather than reveal the structure of your sentence.

What has happened is that the single comma appears now to hide itself, rather than 'the structure of your sentence'.

There is one use of the comma with subordinate clauses that can cause difficulties even for experienced writers. Look at these two sentences:

John admired the car which was in the garage.

John admired the car, which was in the garage.

You can see how the comma alters the meaning. In the first sentence the clause 'which was in the garage' tells us *which* car it was that John admired; we can call this a 'defining' clause. In the second sentence 'which was in the garage' is an additional piece of information about a particular car that, presumably, has already been identified. This we can call a 'describing' clause. It may help you to sort out 'defining' and 'describing' clauses if you remember that *which* can be replaced by *that* in a 'defining' clause but not in a 'describing' clause. For example:

John admired the car that was in the garage.

'Defining' and 'describing' clauses may also begin with such words as *who*, *whose*, *where* and *when*. Here are some examples:

Defining:

The engineer who built the Menai Bridge was Thomas Telford, a man whose work I much admire.

You should do that on a day when there is no wind.

Show me the site where the power station is to be built.

Describing:

Thomas Telford, who was first President of the Institute of Civil Engineers, was without doubt a great engineer.

You can do it on Saturday, when you do not have to go to work.

Exercise 17

See if you can pick out the 'defining' and 'describing' clauses in these sentences:

(a)   I became aware that my pursuer, who by now was only a few yards off, was the man whom I had seen that morning at the inn.

(b)   Last summer I went back to the town where I was born.

(c)   That was in the days when beer was twopence a pint.

(d)   My next trip is to Sheffield, where we are opening a new factory.

Exercise 18

Pick out the wrongly punctuated sentences and correct them. Identify the 'defining' and 'describing' clauses:

(a) People, who live in country districts, are particularly affected by the withdrawal of bus services.

(b) I want you to know the basic rules, which govern punctuation.

(c) The book which I think you should read gives a full account of nuclear power.

(d) It was a letter from my mother who was worried because I had not written lately.

(e) Usually my brother met me at the station, but on that memorable Friday it was my father who came to meet me.

Exercise 19 (revision)

Add commas, a semicolon, full stops and capitals to this passage.

although bats flourish and survive very well today pterodactyls were superseded by birds which have feathers a great many years ago it is possible of course that the extinction of pterodactyls had nothing to do with structural considerations but it is also possible that there is something special about feathers which gives birds an edge over other flying creatures when i worked at the royal aircraft establishment i used to ask my superiors from time to time whether it would not perhaps be better if aeroplanes had feathers but i seldom succeeded in extracting a rational or even a patient answer to this question.

Here are two further points about commas:

1 When writing essays, try to be generous in your use of full stops and sparing in your use of commas. Several short sentences separated by full stops usually provide a more effective means of communicating ideas than one long sentence full of commas.

2 After writing an essay, you should always read through it. If you find a sentence that is ambiguous or does not say quite what you intended, *do not add commas* in an attempt to clarify the meaning. Recast the sentence or break it down into shorter ones.

The apostrophe

The apostrophe is used to indicate possession of a thing or quality by someone or something:

Thing possessed		Possessor	Form using apostrophe
the complexity	of	the system	the system's complexity
the components	of	the mechanism	the mechanism's components
the drawings	of	the architect	the architect's drawings
the drawings	of	the architects	the architects' drawings
the drawings	of	the children	the children's drawings
the charter	of	the university	the university's charter
the aims	of	the course	the course's aims
the aperture	of	the lens	the lens's aperture
the apertures	of	the lenses	the lenses' apertures

It is possible to make a possessive form of a singular word by adding *'s*, but in some cases it should be avoided. For example, it is better to write *the simplicity of the synthesis* than *the synthesis's simplicity*.

The possessive form of plural words sometimes causes difficulty. If the word forms its plural regularly, by adding *-s* or *-es*, then the possessive form has just an apostrophe after the *s*: *architects'*, *lenses'*. *Children*, however, is the plural of *child* and forms its possessive by adding *'s*: *children's*. Other plural possessive forms ending in *'s* include *men's* and *women's*. *People* is an interesting case. It is often treated as a plural, although of course it has a plural of its own (*peoples*). This seems to cause confusion about the form of the possessive. The possessive of *people* is *people's*.

Try not to confuse the process of forming a possessive with that of forming a plural. For example, you know that *university* has *universities* as its plural, but do not let that mislead you into thinking that in the possessive form of the singular the *-y* has to be replaced by *-ie* before you add *'s*. You simply add *'s* to university: *university's*.

Exercise 20

Rewrite these phrases using apostrophes:

(a) the gain of the amplifier

(b) the gains of the amplifiers

(c) the importance of chemistry

(d) the properties of the gas

(e) the properties of the gases

(f) the occupations of the men

An apostrophe is also used to show where a letter or letters have been missed out:

it's	it is	don't	do not
you'll	you will	they're	they are
he's	he is	isn't	is not

Apostrophes are used in this way only to represent direct speech or when writing in a 'conversational' style. There is probably little use for such a style in an essay.

The apostrophe is similarly used to show where figures have been missed out, especially in dates:

a '59 Morris Minor

I haven't been there since '89

Apostrophes are *not* used to form plurals of initials, abbreviations or figures. The plural of *MP*, for example, is *MPs*, that of *e.m.f.* is *e.m.f.s*, and *sixes and sevens* is written with figures as *6s and 7s*. Initials such as MP, BBC or OU form possessives in the regular way. Here is an example:

The BBC's response to the MP's criticisms was to invite the MPs to take part in a discussion programme on broadcasting in the 1990s.

It's and *its*

It's easy to confuse these two.

It's means *it is* (the apostrophe indicating that a letter has been left out):

It's a long way to Tipperary.

Its denotes possession:

The car had its front wheels in the ditch.

Exercise 21

Fill in the blanks with *it's* or *its*:

(a) _____ roof was insulated.

(b) _____ too early for the pubs to be open.

(c) I must have overloaded _____ circuits.

(d) _____ main disadvantage is _____ weight.

(e) _____ the latest model and _____ performance is second to none.

(f) _____ not easy to understand relativity theory because _____ concepts are mathematical.

Parentheses and brackets

The word 'parentheses' is properly used to refer to curved brackets ( ) that are used to insert additional information into a sentence:

Initially, the simple sugar, glucose (Figure 1), is synthesized in leaves by the action of sunlight.

The term 'brackets' is properly used to refer to square brackets [ ] that are used to enclose words or phrases that are added to a text or quoted passage for the purpose of clarification or editorial comment:

He cited the lawyer's opinion that 'the man on the train [Mr Jenkins] must have been provoked beyond endurance'.

It is entirely acceptable to use the term 'brackets' to describe both types of enclosures, qualifying it with the words 'round' or 'square' when necessary.

Note that the singular of 'parentheses' is 'parenthesis'. 'Parenthesis' refers to the word, clause or passage that is contained by the parentheses. Thus someone might say:

It is a matter of concern that the most important point in the whole document appears only as a parenthesis in the final paragraph.

A long parenthesis is surely rather confusing for the reader, since the parentheses are so far apart.

Parentheses are useful for introducing an abbreviation you intend to use later:

You should write to the World Health Organization (WHO) about safety regulations for laboratories, as it is important to comply with WHO's standards.

Parentheses are also used for expressing quantities in an alternative way and for adding dates:

It will be a mild afternoon, with temperatures rising to 15 °C (60 °F).

A masonry arch can span about 200 feet (60 metres) without much difficulty.

Let us begin at the beginning with Newton (1642–1727), who said that action and reaction are equal and opposite.

When parentheses are used in a sentence at the point where another punctuation mark is needed (e.g. the comma in the last example), the other punctuation mark follows the round bracket that closes the parenthesis.

Use parentheses sparingly, making sure that the information contained in them is brief and to the point. Do not use them in an essay for chatty asides or for important points. Here is an example of bad practice:

Among the advantages cited in favour of the 'pricing' approach are claims that it would be administratively cheaper to operate, that it would be fairer (because it would leave decisions with the people who know what's economically and commercially possible), and that it would be more flexible (because it would be relatively simple to increase 'prices' for pollutants which were giving rise to special concern).

Exercise 23

Add parentheses and commas to this passage:

'Polychlorinated biphenyls PCBs should be regarded as if they were carcinogenic to humans' says a report by the International Agency for Research on Cancer *IARC Monographs*, vol. 18. But the authoritative and cautious IARC says there is insufficient evidence to decide whether polybrominated biphenyls PBBs the close chemical cousins of PCBs are also carcinogenic.

Note In mathematics, parentheses and brackets are used in different and precise ways. You learn the rules for those specific uses as you learn mathematics.

Exercise 24 (revision)

Add *parentheses*, commas, full stops and capitals to this passage.

figure 16 shows the pattern of energy flow in the united kingdom in 1975 gross consumption of *primary energy* in the united kingdom was approximately 2425 TW h 1 TW h = 10^9kW h but because of inefficiencies in energy conversion and distribution some 30 per cent or so 725 TW h is lost between producer and consumer even when this *delivered energy* finally arrives at the point of consumption further losses of around 30 per cent 725 TW h occur in the appliances and processes in which it is used central-heating boilers for instance have efficiencies of only 60 per cent or so open coal fires are even worse with a typical efficiency of only 20 per cent and motor cars with internal combustion engines are still less efficient less than 20 per cent.

The hyphen

The prime function of the hyphen is to prevent ambiguity. Its main use is to link the parts of compound words:

mother-in-law, co-opt, cross-section, pro-American, frying-pan, test-tube, wing-span.

Hyphens are used when numbers are written out in full:

fifty-seven, nine-tenths, one hundred and forty-four, six and seven-eights.

The hyphen is used to form compound adjectives:

high-rise flats, a water-cooled engine, a ten-storey office block, long-term planning, twentieth-century technology.

Notice that the need for a hyphen will depend on what your meaning is:

There was a queue of twenty three-ton lorries.	They have a fleet of twenty-three-ton lorries.
There must be a short circuit somewhere.	You cannot short-circuit it without blowing the fuse.
Your subscriptions are not up to date.	Have you got an up-to-date timetable?

A hyphen is sometimes needed with prefixes such as *re-*, *co-*, *pre-*, *sub-*. The following examples illustrate some of the cases that require a hyphen. In many cases you will need to refer to your dictionary for help.

(a) To avoid a doubled letter or other combination that might be misread:

re-erect	but	rebuild
pre-existing	but	preoccupied
sub-basement	but	subcontinent
co-author	but	cosine

(b) With *re-*, to indicate that it is being added to something that is being done again, rather than forming part of a well-known compound word. For example:

The ladies' darts team has been re-formed.

Other examples are: re-cover, re-create

(c) Again with *re-*, the hyphen is used to emphasize the idea of repetition. Compare these two sentences:

You may need to redraw your rough sketches before sending them with your assignment.

I have drawn and re-drawn this diagram, but I cannot get it right.

(d) Finally, less familiar words formed with a prefix may need a hyphen, whereas a well-established word will not. Again, you will find your dictionary of great help. Here are a couple of examples:

pre-scientific	but	prehistoric
ultra-careful	but	ultraviolet light

39

Exercise 26 (revision)

Add punctuation (capitals, commas, a colon, full stops, parentheses and *hyphens*) to this passage:

on the other hand the *unit* costs or 'run on costs' of printing the magazine on a hand operated duplicating machine will be relatively high for various reasons

(a)   the machine because it is hand operated can produce relatively few copies per hour so the labour cost of each copy is relatively high

(b)   the machine for technical reasons has to use fairly heavy paper which makes the cost of each copy relatively high also the stencil being made of waxed paper will break up after say a thousand copies or so and a new one will have to be typed

(c)   the machine prints only one page at a time so that when all the sheets thirty two of them for a sixty four page magazine are finally printed it takes a long time to collate them by hand and staple them into a magazine

---

The dash

It is tempting to think of the dash as an all-purpose punctuation mark. Avoid this temptation. The use of numerous dashes is usually a sign of poorly structured writing. If you find you are sprinkling dashes on the page, ask yourself whether your sentence construction is under control. It is possible to write lively, well-punctuated English without using dashes at all.

Dashes do have accepted uses. In pairs, dashes mark a parenthesis:

(a)   No one has yet built a living organism – however simple – starting from scratch.

(b)   A combination of three types of study – two on humans and one on animals – is a strong indication that alcohol is harmful to unborn babies.

In this kind of use of pair of dashes acts as a 'weak' pair of parentheses. A pair of commas would separate the parenthesis even more weakly.

Exercise 27

Rewrite the above examples using brackets and then commas in place of the dashes. For each sentence, try to decide which punctuation best fits its sense.

A dash may also introduce an explanation or development of the point that comes immediately before:

(a)   The Chinese are thrifty people – the excavated earth was used to make bricks for the tunnel walls.

(b)   Already it has sold six systems – three in Denmark, two in Spain and one in Italy.

Here the dash is being used as if it were a colon.

Exercise 28

Replace the dashes in the above examples with colons. Do you think this an improvement?

Exercise 29

Look at the following passage and try to decide what is the function of each dash. Then try to replace the dashes with other punctuation marks.

A purely inorganic compound with optical activity – the first for almost 50 years – has just been synthesized by Robert Gillard and Franz Winmer of University College, Cardiff. Most known optically active compounds – molecules with structures that cannot be superimposed upon their mirror images – contain carbon atoms. They are either organic compounds, or chelates – complexes of transition metals where the carbon atoms help form the claw-like ligands.

New Scientist, vol. 87, no. 1137 (11 January 1979), p. 92

There are some other uses for dashes. As you will come across them in your reading, you need to understand how they are used.

The uses of closed-up dashes are as follows:

(a) To indicate a link or a non-grammatical relation between two words:

parent–teacher association   cost–benefit analysis
a north–south direction   Labour–Liberal alliance

Near the village of Watford in Northamptonshire the London–Yorkshire motorway (the M1) and the main London–Glasgow railway line run alongside each other for two or three miles.

Classical 'wet' chemical analyses include gravimetric methods, acid–base titrations and oxidation–reduction reactions.

For a nuclear reaction, the separate conservation laws for mass and energy are replaced by a single law of conservation of mass–energy.

The Heisenberg uncertainty principle arises from the dual particle–wave nature of matter.

(b) To indicate a range of values or the extent of a period:

Stainless steel contains 70–90 per cent iron, 12–20 per cent chromium and 0.1–0.7 per cent carbon.

Telford (1757–1834) – the 'Colossus of roads', or 'Pontifex Maximus', as Southey called him – probably built more bridges than anyone else in history.

The best time for sowing a lawn is September–October.

(c) When something is named jointly after two people:

In the Siemens–Martin process, steel is made by melting roughly equal quantities of pig-iron and scrap steel with some iron ore.

The Gieger–Müller tube will detect any type of ionizing particle or radiation.

Exercise 30 (revision)

Add punctuation and capitals to the following:

(a) it is found that meteors fall into two distinct classes the stony and the iron nickel types with a few intermediate or stony iron types

(b) the beer lambert law is an extension of a law proposed by lambert in 1760 which stated that layers of equal thickness of a homogeneous material absorb equal proportions of light

(c) einstein suggested that the path of a particle in four dimensional space time is a geodesic

---

3   Spelling

Many English words are difficult to spell correctly because they are not pronounced in a way that makes the spelling clear. Most people do spell most words correctly, but there are many words that are commonly misspelt. It is these we shall be dealing with in what follows.

If you know you are poor at spelling or you try these exercises and find unfamiliar words that are difficult for you, do keep your dictionary to hand and refer to it constantly. As you will see, there are few rules for spelling. The best way to learn how to spell is to check with a dictionary and then to test yourself repeatedly until you are so familiar with a word that you are sure of its spelling.

Double letters

It is generally clear from the sound of a word whether or not a vowel (a, e, i, o or u) should be doubled:

compare *red* with *reed*, and *hot* with *hoot*.

It is only *e* and *o* that are commonly doubled.

Doubling a consonant (a letter that is not a vowel) does not have such an obvious effect on pronunciation. As a result, it is easy to be confused about when to double consonants.

It is particularly difficult to know whether or not to double a consonant in a verb to which *-ing* or *-ed* is being added. For example, does *drop* become *droping* or *dropping*, *droped* or *dropped*? Here *dropping* and *dropped* are correct; the *p* is doubled. But what happens to the *p* in *droop* and *drape*? In both these verbs the *p* is not doubled. The correct forms are *drooping* and *drooped*, and *draping* and *draped*.

For words like these there is a simple general rule which you may find helpful; but it has some exceptions. The rule is:

Double a single final consonant if the word is pronounced as a short sound (e.g. *drop*), but do not double the final consonant if the word is pronounced as a long sound (e.g. *droop*, *drape*).

Here are some examples:

Short sound
get, getting;   win, winning;   mat, matting, matted

Long sound
gain, gaining, gained;   meet, meeting;   state, stating, stated

The same rule can be used for adjectives, that is, 'describing' words, when writing the forms that end with *-er* and *-est*. For example:

hot, hotter, hottest
sweet, sweeter, sweetest
white, whiter, whitest

It is usually longer words that cause problems. For longer verbs there is another rule, which also relates to the way the word is spoken:

Double a single final consonant if the stress falls at the end of the word, but do not double the final consonant if the stress falls elsewhere.

Here are two examples where the stress falls at the end of the word and the final consonant is doubled:

omit, omitting, omitted
infer, inferring, inferred

In the next examples, the stress falls at the beginning of the word and the final consonant is not doubled:

bias, biasing biased
focus, focusing, focused
offer, offering, offered
visit, visiting, visited

A notable exception to this rule is that in English (as distinct from American) usage, verbs like this that end with a single *-l* have the final *-l* doubled:

travel, travelling, travelled
model, modelling, modelled

The only really safe rule, of course, is: *Look it up in your dictionary.*

Exercise 31

Complete these sentences by adding the correct ending in the blanks.

(a)   Please begin at the begin_____.

(b)   The council has allot_____ a larger proportion of its budget to technical education.

(c)   History will show how much we have benefit_____ from the silicon chip.

(d)   His argument was so compel_____ that we all ended by agreeing with him.

Some words have double consonants that follow no rule and can only be learnt through practice.

Exercise 32

Here is a list of ten words, three of which are spelt correctly. The others should have doubled consonants which have not been doubled here. First, identify the correct words, then rewrite correctly those that are incorrect. When you have finished check with your dictionary.

Word   *Right/Wrong*   *Correct spelling*

(a)   sucesful

(b)   acoustic

(c)   ocasionaly

(d)   comitee

(e)   exagerate

(f)   abreviate

(g)   paralel

(h)   omision

(i)   procedure

(j)   develop

ei and *ie*

At school you probably learnt the rule: '*i* before *e* except after *c* when the sound is *ee*'. Of course, there are exceptions such as *seize*. Again, always remember to check with your dictionary.

Exercise 33

Choose the correct spelling in each sentence.

(a) He achieved/acheived success through hard work.

(b) A quotient/quoteint is the number obtained when one number is divided by another.

(c) The workmanship was so deficeint/deficient that the council refused to accept the property.

(d) Black beams in the cieling/ceiling gave the room an atmosphere of age.

(e) The way we percieve/perceive ourselves affects our relations with other people.

-er and *-or*

Both *-er* and *-or* endings are found in words that describe people in terms of what they do or what their occupation is. For example:

actor, tailor, decorator, collector, donor
painter, butcher, reader, angler, gardener

The ending *-or* is found in words for *things* that do something, for example,

generator, motor, incinerator, radiator

but watch out for exceptions such as *computer* and *propeller*.

Exercise 34

Decide which of these words are spelt correctly, give the correct spelling for the others and check with your dictionary before looking at the answers.

Word	Right/Wrong	Correct spelling
(a) consumer		
(b) accelerater		
(c) manufacturer		
(d) inventer		
(e) distributer		
(f) designer		

-ant and *-ent*; *-ance* (*-ancy*) and *-ence* (*-ency*)

There is no reliable way of telling if a word ends in *-ant* or *-ent*, because the sounds of these endings are not clearly distinguished. However, if the word ends with *-ent* in one form, the other form will end with *-ence* or *-ency*. For example:

frequent	frequency
intelligent	intelligence

If the ending is *-ant*, the related ending is *-ance* or *-ancy*. For example:

important	importance
tolerant	tolerance
infant	infancy

Exercise 35

Complete these sentences by adding the missing letters to the words.

(a)   All chemical elements and compounds are subst_____s, but solutions are mixtures.

(b)   If there had been any recurr_____ of the events, the club would have been closed.

(c)   The infer_____s drawn from the market-research data proved correct.

(d)   The properties and dimensions of a piece of material determine its electrical resist_____.

(e)   It is too soon to evaluate the perform_____ of the new equipment.

-ious, *-ous* and *-eous*

The endings *-ious*, *-ous* and *-eous* are all used to make adjectives and they are often confused. The pair *-ious* and *-eous* cause the most problems because they sound the same. For example, listen to the sounds of these words:

   precious, herbaceous   courteous, dubious   hideous, curious

There are no rules for these endings. The correct endings must be learnt. Note carefully, please, the spelling of *mischievous*.

48

-*able* and -*ible*

Adjectives can be formed from verbs by adding an -*able* or an -*ible*
ending. For example:

accept	acceptable
advise	advisable
digest	digestible
reverse	reversible

There are many rules for deciding which ending a word should have.
Here are some simple ones; but remember they do not cover every
occasion.

If the part of the word before the ending is a complete word (perhaps
with a final mute *e*), the ending is probably -*able*. For example:

love	lovable
advise	advisable
tax	taxable

Words ending in -*ce* or -*ge* should retain the -*e* before adding -*able*. For
example:

pronounce	pronounceable
manage	manageable
change	changeable

49

If the part of the word before the ending is not complete, the ending is often *-ible*. For example:

horrible, edible, feasible

There are several exceptions to this rule, however. For example:

accessible, reversible, contemptible

Exercise 37

Choose the correctly spelt word from those offered in each sentence. Remember to check with your dictionary.

(a)   Fine food and agreeable/agreeible/agreable company make for a pleasant evening.

(b)   Haste is no excuse for illegable/illegible writing.

(c)   As the fog cleared, the ship became visable/visible on the horizon.

(d)   Children's toys should be made of durable/durible materials.

(e)   The system is flexable/flexible enough to allow for delays in production.

(f)   All cars must be fitted with adjustable/adjustible seat belts.

-ary and *-ery*

Here is a useful guide (not a rigid rule).

Words ending in *-ery* are usually nouns, that is, 'naming' words, and contain a complete smaller word within them. For example:

Noun	*Smaller word*
confectionery	confection
discovery	discover
stationery	stationer

Words ending in *-ary* are usually adjectives. For example:

documentary, tributary, stationary

Note that *library* is an exception.

Exercise 38

Examine this list of words and decide in each case whether the missing letter is *e* or *a*; then write the correct spelling in the space provided.

(a) bin__ry _____

(b) machin__ry _____

(c) necess__ry _____

(d) contempor__ry _____

(e) periph__ry _____

(f) deliv__ry _____

(g) prim__ry _____

Have you checked your answers with your dictionary?

-sion and *-tion*

Words ending in *-sion* and *-tion* are usually nouns formed from verbs. Some guidance about which ending to use may be obtained by studying the ending of the verb from which the noun is formed.

A noun ending in *-sion* is formed from verbs ending in:

-nd	(expand, expansion)
-de	(provide, provision)
-ss	(discuss, discussion)
-mit	(omit, omission)
-pel	(propel, propulsion – note the *u*)
-vert	(divert, diversion)

A noun ending in *-tion* is formed from verbs ending in:

-ct	(act, action)
-te	(create, creation)
-pose	(dispose, disposition)

Exercise 39

Make nouns with *-sion* or *-tion* endings from the following words:

(a) extend _____   (d) transmit _____

(b) distribute _____   (e) restrict _____

(c) repulse _____   (f) construct _____

-ceed, -cede and -sede

Words with these endings cause confusion. There is no rule for their spelling. Words ending in *-ceed* and *-cede* come from the same Latin stem, meaning 'to go' or 'to yield', and have simply changed spelling through time. *Supersede* is the only word in English to end in *-sede*.

exceed	accede	supersede
proceed	concede	
succeed	intercede	
	precede	
	recede	
	secede	

Exercise 40

A list of dictionary meanings is given. Write the correct word from the above lists next to the meaning, then check in your own dictionary.

(a) to go on, or continue   _____

(b) to replace   _____

(c) to go before   _____

(d) to achieve something   _____

Exercise 41

Here are a few more words people sometimes have problems with. Choose the correct spelling and write it at the side. Then check with your dictionary.

(a) asertain/assertain/ascertain   _____

(b) miscellaneous/miscelaneous/miscelanous   _____

(c) consious/consciouse/conscious   _____

(d) disciplin/disipline/discipline   _____

(e) artificial/artifisial/artifitial   _____

(f) oficial/ofitial/official   _____

(g) escential/essential/esential   _____

(h) inisial/initial/inishal   _____

Remember that you may have a problem with a word simply because it is an exception to a rule. When in doubt: *Use your dictionary*.

4 Grammar

Sentence structure

Most sentences contain a subject and an associated verb, that is, a 'being' or 'doing' word. The subject is the person or thing that is doing the doing or being. Here is an example of a complete sentence:

> In the summer of 1991 the Soviet Union applied for full membership of the International Monetary Fund.

'The Soviet Union' is the subject of the sentence. 'Applied' is the verb.
If I wanted to add further information to the sentence I could do so in two ways. I could add a phrase:

> In the summer of 1991 the Soviet Union applied for full membership of the International Monetary Fund, seeking access to cash from the Fund.

Or I could construct two short sentences, each with its own subject and verb:

> In the summer of 1991 the Soviet Union applied for full membership of the International Monetary Fund. Full membership gives access to cash from the Fund.

If you think that your sentences seem long and clumsy, break them into shorter sentences, but always make sure that each one contains a main subject and verb.

Exceptions to sentences containing a subject and verb are generally used to achieve a particular effect, as in slogans and commands. When writing your assignments, essays and study notes you are not in the business of giving commands; nor are slogans appropriate.

Which of the examples below are complete sentences? For each complete sentence, write down the subject and its associated verb. Rewrite the non-sentences. (Your rewritten sentences may differ from those in the Answer section at the back of this book but try to check that there is a main subject and a main verb in each.)

(a)   The related concepts of force and inertia in physics.

(b)   Worms and insects which live in the soil.

(c)   More than a hundred years ago, John Stuart Mill realized that industrial society, by its very nature, could not last for long and that the stable society that must replace it would be far better.

(d)   From the statement that the whole is greater than the sum of its parts, it follows that the parts are simpler than the whole.

(e)   A natural cycle for every element needed for life, each with its own natural circulation rate.

(f) Pollution from getting rid of wastes at the least possible cost.

(g) Gaseous emissions may well become a significant problem as breeder reactors and fuel-reprocessing plants come into operation.

(h) Generating electric currents from mechanical motion and hence of converting mechanical energy to electrical.

(i) The rate of technological advancement has always been determined by our discovery and manipulation of materials to meet our needs.

(j) The process of cracking, by which large molecules are broken down into smaller ones by means of high temperatures and pressures.

(k) Soil deterioration and eventually erosion by intensification of farming.

(l) Although it is true to say that maintenance, wear and tear, and petrol costs are fairly closely related to the time spent travelling, it seems that many motorists make decisions about a journey on the basis of average fuel costs per mile.

Prepositions

A preposition is a word used with a noun (or noun equivalent) to relate the noun to some other word:

We walked *up* the path, *along* the ridge and *down* the farm track.

Other examples of prepositions are:

in, over, across, with, for, upon

For example:

to take an interest *in*
to be contingent *upon*

English is particularly rich in prepositions. Judiciously used, they help us to give our thoughts precise expression. Make sure you use the correct preposition. Here are some examples of incorrect and correct uses.

It seemed *like* the whole country was on holiday.	(incorrect)
It seemed *as if* the whole country was on holiday.	(correct)
I am different *than* my sister.	(incorrect)
I am different *from* my sister.	(correct)
I have been suffering *with* bronchitis this winter.	(incorrect)
I have been suffering *from* bronchitis this winter.	(correct)

Exercise 43

What is wrong with each of these sentences? Write the correct sentences in the spaces provided.

(a) Stainless steel consists in carbon steel with nickel and chromium added.

(b) I had scarcely begun the calculations than my calculator batteries went flat.

(c) Will you join me in a pint?

(d) The strike was called to protest at the low bonus offered.

(e) All applicants will be judged on their knowledge of management techniques.

Pronouns

Confusion over pronouns (e.g. *me*, *him*, *it*, *you*) often occurs. It happens particularly in the case of 'you and me' or 'you and I'. Should it be 'She gave it to my brother and me' or 'She gave it to my brother and I'? The former is correct.

The best way to decide whether you should write *I* or *me*, *he* or *him*, *she* or *her*, *they* or *them*, when there are other people in the sentence, is to imagine the sentence with the other people left out (if that is possible). For example:

Please allocate the work to Lucy and I.

Please allocate the work to I (wrong).

Please allocate the work to me (right).

Exercise 44

Correct these sentences where necessary:

(a) He is afraid of George and I.

(b) George and I are afraid of him and her.

(c) He gave it to both me and he.

(d) Between you and I, he probably won't come.

(e) A quarrel arose between him and me.

A note on *like*

I cannot recall all the formulae like I used to.

In that sentence the word 'like' is being used incorrectly as a joining word. The sentence should be either:

I cannot recall all the formulae as I used to.

Or

I cannot recall all the formulae in the way (that) I used to.

You may find it helpful:

(a)   to associate *like* with a noun (*like* somebody, something). For example:

Nothing succeeds like success.

(b)   to associate *as* with a verb (in a similar manner or way). For example:

Nothing succeeds as success does.

Agreement of verb with subject

You saw in earlier examples and exercises that the main subject and its associated verb often become separated from each other. They should always agree in number; that is to say, a singular subject should always take a singular verb and a plural subject a plural verb.

Look at the following sentences. Which are the main subjects and verbs in them? Does each verb agree in number with its subject?

The strength and ductility of a solid depends on how easily cracks will occur.

The presence of such substances as carbon, silicon and sulphur affect the behaviour of cast iron.

The first example is incorrect. It has a double subject, 'strength and ductility', and so a plural form of the verb is required: *depend*.

The second sentence is also incorrect. The subject of the sentence is 'presence' and so a singular form of the verb is required: *affects*.

When using the verb 'to be' (I am, you are, etc.), be especially vigilant over the agreement of verb with subject when you have a singular subject and a plural predicate. For example:

A special *feature* of the series *is* the individual ratings given for quality, price and best recent vintages.

Here are some more examples to illustrate the point:

In the mid-nineteenth century, included among particularly unhealthy trades, *was* the Midlands hardware *industry* in and around Birmingham.

In the mid-nineteenth century, included among particularly unhealthy trades, *were* the Midlands hardware *factories*.

In the mid-nineteenth century, the Midlands hardware *industry* *was* one of the particularly unhealthy trades.

Exercise 45

Correct the following sentences:

(a)   The amount of viscosity exhibited by different fluids vary.

(b)   So much water and oil has been drawn from underground that the resources are much depleted.

(c)   A library of subroutines contribute to the value of a computer installation in much the same way as an extra piece of equipment would do.

(d)   The limitation of exhaust emissions and atmospheric pollution generally by the application of smoke control regulations are a further step in the improvement of the road-user's environment.

(e)   The dotted curves in the figure show the distribution of population in the previous ten years.

Too many prepositions

It is common for people to add unnecessary prepositions. Here are some examples:

Our theatre seats were very near to the orchestra.

In this example *near* is enough on its own; *to* should be left out:

Our theatre seats were very near the orchestra.

We always help old people off of the bus.   (*of* is unnecessary)

We spent most of our holidays inside of the caravan.   (*of* is unnecessary)

Prepositions are sometimes added unnecessarily to verbs:

The fuel tank was emptied out.   (*out* is implied in *emptied*)

In the first part of the course, you will be studying about the effects of technology on your own life.   (*about* is unnecessary)

Connect the inlet pipe up with the tap.   (*up* is unnecessary)

In these examples the extra preposition is redundant and should be omitted.

Exercise 46

What is wrong with each of these sentences? For each sentence, mark the unnecessary word.

(a)   The cost of food has risen steadily ever since the 1990 changes in the CAP.

(b)   She suffered a broken leg when she was knocked off of her bike.

(c)   Being as this tutorial will finish so late, there'll be no time for a drink.

(d)   There were approximately about ten per cent more students this year.

(e)   It took three days by air to reach Australia up until Concorde flew that route.

Ending sentences

Do not use a preposition to end a sentence with.

Do you agree with this advice?
There is probably no need to point out that the sentence itself breaks its own rule. A better version is:

Do not end a sentence with a preposition.

Sir Ernest Gowers advises, 'Do not hesitate to end a sentence with a preposition if your ear tells you that that is where the preposition goes best.' (*The Complete Plain Words*, p. 106) In some sentences it is almost impossible not to end with a preposition. For example:

His head should be cut off.

Look at what you're standing on.

I give up.

Exercise 47

Rewrite the following sentences so that the preposition does not occur at the end.

(a) What have you given it to me for?

(b) It was their new house that I was envious of.

(c) When I began the journey I was unsure where I was going to.

Affect and *effect*

Affect is mainly used as a verb, and in two senses. In one sense 'to affect' means 'to influence'. For example:

The legislation to protect the environment will *affect* my style of living.

In another sense, 'to affect' means 'to make a show or pretence of'. For example:

I shall *affect* an air of indifference to the whole matter.

Effect can be used either as a verb or as a noun. As a verb it means 'to cause something to happen', 'to bring about something'. For example:

He used a safety pin and a piece of elastic to *effect* a temporary repair.

Here is an example of its use as a noun:

The *effect* of microprocessors at work is to increase the speed with which we deal with correspondence.

Exercise 48

Fill in the gaps in these sentences, using parts of either *affect* or *effect*.

(a) He _____ to be unmoved by the team's criticism.

(b) The measures are designed to _____ the demand on this resource.

(c) The _____ of these measures will be to aid the motorist.

(d) The replacement of the valve was _____ quietly and smoothly.

In the following sentence both affect and effect make sense, but the meanings are different.

Extra training may *affect* his promotion.

This means that the training may influence his promotion.

Extra training may *effect* his promotion.

Here the meaning is that training may bring about his promotion.

Exercise 49

Explain the difference in meaning between these two sentences.

(a) A further adjustment in the position of the equipment will *affect* its quiet running.

(b) A further adjustment in the position of the equipment will *effect* its quiet running.

Singulars, plurals and collective nouns

There are many words that denote a collection of things or people but which are singular in form; for example, *team*, *herd*, *committee*, *council*, *Government*, *Parliament*. These are known as collective nouns. A collective noun may be followed by either a singular or plural verb, depending on whether you are thinking of the collection as a unit or as a group of individual items. For example, you may write either:

The Government has decided to ration petrol.

Or

The Government have decided to ration petrol.

Both sentences are acceptable.

When other words in the sentence, apart from the verb, refer to the collective noun you must be consistent:

(a) The Government *has* decided that *they* will ration petrol.

(b) The Government *have* decided that *they* will ration petrol.

(c) The Government *has* decided that *it* will ration petrol.

(a) is incorrect; (b) and (c) are correct.

As a general rule the following words are used with a singular verb: *neither*, *each*, *either*, *every*. Here are some examples of correct usage:

In the case of particles in a closed container, *each exerts* a small impulse when it collides with the walls of the container.

Either physical or mathematical modelling *is used* to illustrate the behaviour of the system.

Note Both 'none *is*' and 'none *are*' are acceptable.

Sometimes errors occur because it is not immediately apparent whether a subject is singular or plural. In the list below, all the words outside brackets are plurals, although they may not look or sound it. Their singular forms are given inside the brackets.

criteria	(criterion)	strata	(stratum)
bacteria	(bacterium)	media	(medium)
phenomena	(phenomenon)	formulae	(formula)
radii	(radius)		

Note Formulas is an alternative plural form of *formula*.

Media, data and index

Media is the plural of *medium*, except when *medium* is used in a spiritualist sense, as in 'séance mediums'.

Data is a plural word. The singular, *datum*, is found in phrases such as 'datum point', meaning the single point to which other data are compared or related. There is no absolute singular form, but 'one of the data' is acceptable. Do not use *data* simply as a more technical-sounding word for 'information'.

There are two plural forms for the singular *index*.

Indexes are found at the back of books etc., for example, indexes of names, subjects, etc.

Indices is the other plural. It is used in mathematics, economics and generally in technical subjects. Indices in mathematics are the little numbers representing 'powers'. In economics there are indices of retail prices, the cost of living, wages and share prices.

Exercise 50

Correct these sentences where necessary.

(a) The bar graph is used to represent data that is either nominally or ordinally scaled.

(b) It is easy to work out the circumference of a circle once the length of a radii is known.

(c) If neither of these experimental methods are successful you must try a third one.

(d) The committee was divided in their opinions.

(e) In your essays you may write 'none is' or 'none are'; either are acceptable.

(f) Adding the indexes is a method of multiplication in mathematics.

(g) Each of the units of measurement were originally natural units based on the lengths of certain parts of the human hand or foot.

(h) The action of bacterium break down the carbon compounds of plant systems to carbon dioxide and water.

(i) In a White Paper of 1970 a network of motorways for England of 4200 miles were proposed.

(j) What is your criteria for making such a judgement?

(k) The strata of relatively impermeable rocks that lie either above or below confined aquifers are called aquicludes.

(l) Either distribution through microwave radio links, using tall towers, or transmission from a satellite far above the surface of the earth are possible ways of disseminating television.

Confusing pairs of words

Words that are similar to each other in spelling or sound, or both, may sometimes be confused with each other. Use your dictionary if you need to check any meanings among the examples below.

principal	principle
practice	practise
stationary	stationery
diffuse	defuse
compliment	complement
discrete	discreet
precede	proceed

Exercise 51

Choose the correct word from the pair given to complete the following sentences.

(a)   In order to fit in her clarinet practice/practise, she had to miss the children's television programmes.

(b)   Petroleum is the principle/principal raw material for plastic.

(c)   With a practiced/practised flick of his wrist, he threw the crumpled paper into his waste-paper basket.

(d)   Since Liz's accident the team has been one player short of its compliment/complement.

(e)   Libraries should have diffuse/defuse lighting to aid reading.

(f)   I knew I could confide in him because he is always discrete/discreet.

(g)   The article always precedes/proceeds the noun to which it refers.

(h)   The basic principal/principle of successful animal husbandry is quite simple: provide warmth and regular feeding.

(i)   I would like to compliment/complement you on the skills you showed in dealing with the task.

(j)   When London became a target for terrorists, special units of police were trained to diffuse/defuse bombs.

(k)   Monogrammed stationery/stationary is an expensive luxury.

(l)   He managed somehow to collide with a stationery/stationary vehicle.

(m)   Under the instructor's watchful eye she proceeded/preceded to demonstrate Hooke's law.

(n)   A variable that can take only certain values is called a discrete/discreet variable.

Sentence structure: positioning words

We have been considering the essential parts of a sentence: the subject and verb. When other parts of speech are added, the arrangement of the words becomes very important. In the two sentences:

Water can be produced from steam. Steam can be produced from water.

the words are the same, but when they are reversed the meanings of the sentences are reversed too.

The effect on meaning of the positioning of words is not always as obvious as it is in the examples above. In more complex sentences, careful thought is often needed to make sure words are correctly placed in a clearly understandable way.

A helpful hint for constructing complex sentences is to try, where possible, to place words associated together as near as possible to each other.

For example, the word 'only' when used as an adverb (i.e. to modify, or tell more about, the meaning of the verb) should be placed before its associated verb. What do you think this sentence means?

I've only borrowed the books.

The writer may be intending to say either:

It's just the books I've borrowed.

Or

I've merely borrowed the books. (I've not stolen them, thrown them away, etc.)

Since 'only' comes before its verb, the sentence is to be understood as 'I've merely borrowed the books' and the other meaning is better expressed as 'I have borrowed only the books.'

Exercise 52

There are six possible positions for 'only' in the sentence given below. What are they and how is the meaning affected?

I spoke to my tutor yesterday.

Relations within a sentence

In a sentence, always keep items that are closely related in meaning close enough together to avoid doubt or ambiguity. Here is an example of ambiguity:

The boxer aimed a blow at his opponent's jaw, which slipped off and hit him on the shoulder.

Consider writing that sentence unambiguously. It could be written:

The blow, which the boxer had aimed at his opponent's jaw, slipped off and hit his opponent's shoulder.

It is important to place pronouns as near as possible to the nouns they represent, otherwise the meaning can become confused.

Exercise 53

Rewrite these sentences to avoid confusion.

(a)   The shark-spotting helicopter apparently failed to see the shark, although it was circling over the bathers.

(b)   As the guard went about his duties he watched him closely, noting the time he came to feed him.

(c)   I told my mother that she should help her.

(d)   If the baby doesn't thrive on raw milk, boil it.

(e)   There are some sticking plasters in my desk, which I keep for emergencies.

Confusing words

Some words are confused with others because of similarities in their meaning or in the way they are used.

These are three pairs of words often confused:

less	fewer
comprise	constitute
lay	lie

Less refers to amount, quantity or extent, and takes a singular noun. For example:

The profit this year was less than last.

Fewer refers to number and is used with plural nouns. For example:

There are fewer school-leavers without jobs this year.

Comprise is equivalent to *consist of*. For example:

The accommodation offered comprised bedsitting room, kitchen and shared bathroom.

Note that *comprise(d) of* is wrong.

Constitute is equivalent to *compose*. For example:

Twelve people constituted the study group.

Lay means to put, to place or to knock down, and its correct forms are *lay*, *laid*, *laid* (i.e. I might say 'I lay', 'I laid' or 'I have laid'). For example:

Please lay down your pens.

He laid the parcel on the table.

Notice that one always lays *something*.

Lie means to assume a recumbent position or to wait, and its correct forms are *lie*, *lay*, *lain*. For example:

He felt faint and was obliged to lie down.

She lay motionless, sprawled across the threshold.

They have lain in wait for the burglar now for three nights.

Exercise 54

Choose the correct word of those offered.

(a)   There were less/fewer than twenty people present.

(b)   The committee comprised/constituted the president of the club, the secretary, the treasurer and three elected members.

(c)   'I have run ten miles,' he said, and laid/lay/lied down exhausted.

Who and *whom*

Misuse of *who* and *whom* can cause a lot of confusion. The following three rules are offered as guidelines.

Rule 1
Use *who* when it is the subject (the doer) of a verb. For example:
   I wish I knew who wrote it.

Rule 2
Use *whom* when it is the object (the person directly affected by the verb). For example:
   Whom should I see when I arrive?

Rule 3
Use *whom* if it is governed by a preposition (to, from, by, etc.).
For example:
   And therefore never send to know for *whom* the bell tolls.

Exercise 55

Indicate by a tick or a cross whether you think each of these sentences is right or wrong.

(a)   It is he to whom I had given my watch.

(b)   Who have you got that from?

(c)   This sentence is written by someone whom, it appears, is illiterate.

(d)   The tenant, whom we thought to be trustworthy, has burnt the house down.

(e)   Whom do you suppose is coming to tea?

Nouns used as adjectives

It is quite common in modern English to use one noun to *qualify* another; in other words, to use a noun as an adjective. Here are some examples:

   aluminium alloy
   wire bristles
   motor vehicles
   gas cylinder

It has also become commonplace to write strings of nouns together in the style of a newspaper headline rather than to use constructions containing prepositions. Consider the phrase:

a national energy crisis conference

It could be written more clearly as:

a conference on the crisis in national energy (resources)

That example demonstrates one of the shortcomings of this style of writing, in which conciseness is gained at the expense of a clear indication of the exact relations between the words in the phrases. Here is another example:

the world food production situation

which might mean:

the amount and kinds of food produced throughout the world

although what, if anything, 'situation' means in this phrase is an open question. The use of hyphens can sometimes help to achieve clarity. For example:

the world food-production situation

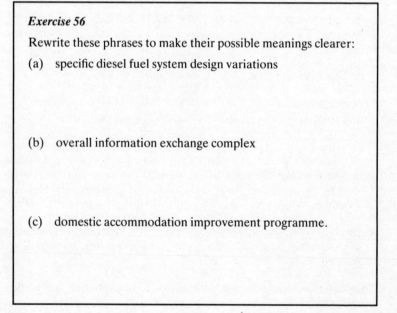

Exercise 56

Rewrite these phrases to make their possible meanings clearer:

(a)   specific diesel fuel system design variations

(b)   overall information exchange complex

(c)   domestic accommodation improvement programme.

Unattached participles

Remember the guidance given earlier. When putting a sentence together, you should try to place its most closely connected words as near each other as possible.

Sometimes words that are intended to modify other words in a sentence are not correctly attached to the words they are meant to modify.

The present participle of a verb has a form ending in *-ing* (like *ending*). The present participle always needs to be attached to some word that it modifies, as 'ending' was attached to 'form'.

Consider this sentence:

Looking out of the window, I saw an old friend walking down the street.

Here it is quite clear who is doing the looking ('I') and who is walking ('an old friend').

Now look at this example:

Crossing the line, a train bumped into him.

In this sentence the writer wanted to say that it was a man who was crossing the line, but the grammar of the sentence suggests it was the train that was crossing the line. 'Crossing' is unattached, that is, it is without a word to which it can refer. The sentence could be altered to read:

As he was crossing the line, a train bumped into him.

Similar problems can occur with the past participle of a verb. A past participle of a verb is not quite so easy to recognize as a present participle. Although many verbs form their past participle with an *-ed* ending (sometimes modified to *-t*), others have past participles ending in *-en* (e.g. *broken*). For lots of common short verbs the past participle is either the same as the simple verb (e.g. *run*, *hit*) or is formed by changing the vowel in the middle (e.g. *hung*, *got*). Here is an example:

Formal application is now being made for the necessary way-leave consent, and as soon as it is received the work will proceed.

The sentence construction is ambiguous. It suggests that the work, not the formal application, is to be received.

Unattached participles are not always as obvious as they are in the examples above. Can you spot and correct what is wrong with these?

(a)   We thank you for your order and, being always anxious to carry out our customers' wishes immediately, would you kindly state the address to which you wish the goods to be delivered.

(b)   Whilst requesting you to furnish the return now outstanding you are advised that in future no further credit will be extended.

(c)   Administered at first by the National Gallery, it was not until 1917 that the appointment of a separate board and director enabled a fully independent policy to be pursued.

(d)   Arising out of a confrontation between the Government and the Opposition over devolution, the Opposition may seek an early vote of no confidence in the Government.

Note Some *-ing* words are now treated as acceptable on their own, that is, unattached. This is usually because the unexpressed subject is indefinite; for example, 'one', 'people'. A few examples of these words are: regarding, considering, owing to, concerning, failing. The following are regarded as acceptable:

Roughly speaking, present participles and gerunds are recognized by their *-ing* endings.

Considering the attack that had been made on him, his speech was moderate in tone.

Double negatives

Double negatives are to be avoided. The two halves of a double negative cancel each other. Thus, 'I didn't see nothing' means 'I did see something,' although the speaker may have intended quite the opposite. If a negative meaning is required the sentence should contain only one negative. The above example should therefore be either 'I saw nothing' or 'I didn't see anything.'

Double negatives can result from the use of 'scarcely' or 'hardly'. Both these words are indirectly negative and should be matched with a positive verb. For example:

There *was* hardly any heating in the office.
('was' is the positive verb)

Not

There *wasn't* hardly any heating in the office.

It is possible to use double negatives correctly. Here is an example of a correct double negative:

It is only those who do nothing who make no mistakes.

This means the same as

Everyone who does something makes mistakes sometimes.

Another kind of double negative makes use of an *un-* formation. Here are two examples:

The design of the building was not unattractive.
I felt not unhappy about my answer.

73

In these examples the double negative does not mean the same as the direct positive, 'attractive' or 'happy'. This kind of double negative should be used very sparingly. Used occasionally it can convey a precise shade of meaning, but repeated use creates an impression of fussiness or pedantry.

Exercise 58

Rewrite these sentences in the positive sense, but in such a way that they retain the literal meaning of the original sentences.

(a)   He wasn't scarcely able to read the book.

(b)   'I didn't say nothing,' she protested.

(c)   It's not an unworkable solution.

(d)   I couldn't not go.

(e)   There is no one in this room who has not sometimes lied.

Split infinitives

The part of the verb called the infinitive is formed in English with *to* plus the verb-word itself (for example, 'to study').

To split or not to split?

It is generally considered ill-advised *to knowingly put* (as I just have) a word or words between the *to* of the infinitive and the verb-word itself. But sometimes the sense of a sentence is made obscure or its expression clumsy through avoiding a split infinitive.

Think about what this sentence means:

He began slowly to introduce new examples.

Is it his beginning that is slow or the introduction of new examples? If the first meaning is wanted, the sentence should be:

He slowly began to introduce new examples.

But if that is not what is meant, it would clarify the meaning to split the infinitive:

He began to slowly introduce new examples.

That is now clear, but so is:

He began to introduce new examples slowly.

Now consider another example:

They decided often to discuss political questions.

Again it might be preferable to split the infinitive, but this can be avoided and the meaning made clearer by writing:

They decided to discuss political questions often.

A split infinitive is only rarely the natural way to convey one's meaning.

Think: Can you move the word that splits the infinitive without changing the meaning? If you can, do so.

Please note:

'To fully understand' is a split infinitive.
'To fully have understood' is a split infinitive.
'To have fully understood' is not a split infinitive.

If you are in doubt, try putting words such as 'fully' after all parts of the verb you are using.

Exercise 59

Correct these sentences as necessary.

(a)   It is the intention of the Minister of Transport to substantially increase all present rates by means of a general percentage.

(b)   We intend to further support attempts at obtaining a truce.

(c)   He seems to still be allowed to speak at demonstrations.

(d)   The greatest difficulty about assessing the economic achievements of the Government is that its spokespersons tend to always exaggerate them.

(e)   The directors are said to strongly favour these reforms.

(f)   It will be possible to considerably improve our working conditions.

---

5 Style

Repetition

Clumsy repetition usually occurs because concentration has lapsed. A word or phrase is repeated in the same sentence, or in the sentence immediately after, in a way that does not clarify the meaning but gives the reader an uncomfortable feeling. For example:

> The lecturer *also* mentioned the importance of the bicycle to the developing emancipation of women. He *also* included some material from an unpublished thesis.

In that example it would be better to omit the first *also*.
Here is another example:

> It is *essential* that you should be familiar with essential theories in the field.

In this case it would be better to change one of the *essentials*. The sentence might be rewritten as:

> It is absolutely necessary that you should be familiar with essential theories in the field.

> Look at this example:

> The increase in demand for *liquid oxygen* in the 1950s prompted the building of larger vehicles to carry the *liquid oxygen*.

Here it is better to replace the repeated phrase with a pronoun:

> The increase in demand for liquid oxygen in the 1950s prompted the building of larger vehicles to carry it.

> When you are thinking about replacing a noun, that is, a 'naming' word, with a pronoun, always check that there can be no doubt about which noun the pronoun stands for. Avoid ambiguities of the following kind:

> He placed the file next to the library book so that he would not forget it.

Exercise 60

Rewrite the following sentences so that repetition is avoided:

(a) Because I was late with my work because I found the calculations difficult, I didn't know whether my tutor would mark it.

(b) The Prime Minister went on to say that it was hoped that everyone would support the new environmental measures. Backbenchers went on to give the scheme unqualified support.

(c) If there is anything further I can do in the next few weeks to further the project, I will do it.

Latin phrases

There is nothing greatly superior about Latin phrases but their use is well established and you will come across them again and again in your reading. It's as well, therefore, to know the meanings of the most-used Latin phrases so that you understand them and can use them correctly in your own writing if you wish.

Some of the best-known Latin phrases are used in abbreviated form. Below are three of the most common ones, together with the full Latin in brackets and the English meaning.

i.e. (*id est*)	that is
etc. (*et cetera*)	and other things
e.g. (*exempli gratia*)	for example

Here are three examples of the use of each, with the English equivalent shown in brackets:

When working with any metal you must be aware of its various properties: malleability, conductivity, hardness, etc. (and other things).

Metal for forging must be malleable and ductile, i.e. (that is) able to be shaped without cracking when heated.

Metals used in forging are usually ferrous, e.g. (for example) wrought iron.

It's important to understand that *i.e.* (that is) and *e.g.* (for example) are not interchangeable. The proper use of *e.g.* is to introduce *an example or examples*, as in this sentence:

We need to be given more details of the accident, e.g. whether the operator was wearing the correct protective clothing.

On the other hand, *i.e.* introduces *another way of saying* what has already been said, driving home or clarifying the point that has been made:

Do not use the components from this sealed box until absolutely necessary, i.e. when all other components have been used.

Exercise 61

Write the correct Latin abbreviations in the gaps in these sentences.

(a)   Although different units of length – kilometre, centimetre, millimetre, _____ – are in common use, all your linear measurements should be given in metres.

(b)   Computers are used extensively in business to deal with routine and repetitive tasks, _____ lower-level clerical work.

(c)   It is very often possible to draw opposite conclusions from the same facts because they have to be interpreted, _____ given meaning by the people observing them.

(d)   The strike caused many inconveniences; _____ the refuse was not collected.

(e)   If we are to take action, we need proof of his having been party to the contract, _____ we need documentary or other conclusive evidence.

Redundancy

Redundancy is more difficult to detect than repetition because it is dependent on the meanings of the words, not just on the repeating of a of a word. Redundancy is a superfluity or excess; in writing, it is the use of more words than necessary to express the required meaning.

Take this example:

I shall continue to remain here.

'Continue' is implied in 'remain', so this sentence would be better as:

I shall remain here.

Here is another example:

There are desirable benefits to be gained from increasing research into alternative energy sources.

Benefits *are* desirable things, so 'desirable' is redundant.

Now consider these two sentences:

There is something about nuclear power stations that provokes anxiety.

There were a number of us who disagreed with your argument.

Beginning a sentence with a phrase like 'there is' or 'there were' often contributes nothing to its meaning. The following constructions are better:

Something about nuclear power stations provokes anxiety.

A number of us disagreed with your argument.

Exercise 62

Pick out any words or phrases that are redundant in these sentences and rewrite where necessary.

(a) An attempt will be made today to try to achieve a settlement.

(b) There is a possibility that the mortar will crack.

(c)   British people have never before in the past suffered so much from the effects of overeating.

(d)   The building was constructed from modules, square in shape and all of the same dimensions.

(e)   The subject of the discussion is about the role of Government in scientific advance.

(f)   The electrician explained the reason for the short in the circuit was because the water had dropped on to the wires.

Non-sexist language

The careful reader will probably be aware of sexist language used extensively in everyday life, in both written and spoken forms. One of the many reasons for not using sexist language is that it often confuses meaning and so is not plain English. At all times try to use non-sexist language that makes your meaning clear and avoids clumsiness and inconsistency.

Here are some examples of obvious sexist words and phrases and their non-sexist alternatives:

man (generic), mankind	humankind, human race, people
man the desk	staff the desk
man-made	synthetic, machine-made

Try to avoid being unnecessarily gender-specific:

A cat's silent stalking helps *him* to catch prey.

A cat's silent stalking helps *it* to catch prey.

Look out for adjectives and metaphors that imply gender characteristics:

He put up a *manly* fight against overwhelming odds.

He put up a *courageous* fight against overwhelming odds.

Women are sometimes referred to as if they are the subordinates to, or possessions of, men. For example:

man and wife   husband and wife

Mrs Kathleen Gray, wife of Mr Frank Gray, is giving a second series of lectures in the autumn . . . (delete 'wife of Mr Frank Gray').

Job titles sometimes reveal gender assumptions. For example:

foreman	supervisor
watchman	guards
middleman	contact, go-between

The more you use non-sexist alternatives the easier it becomes to do so. You may find your early attempts are rather clumsy but it is always possible, by changing words or the order of words, to work out a clear and natural sentence or phrase. Consider how this is done in the following example:

He or she may have something on his/her mind.

He or she may be worried about something.

Often the cause of stress is that the manager herself or himself, is not quite sure of his or her objectives. She or he then passes on this confusion to his or her staff.

Manager's may be stressed because they are unaware or their own objectives. They then pass on this confusion to their staff.

It is not uncommon nowadays for textbook authors to vary the references to females and males in alternate chapters; but this is rarely done in juxtaposition as in the example given above.

If you are in doubt about non-sexist alternatives, please refer to one of the various publications on non-sexist language.

Exercise 63

Find an alternative way of expressing any sexist language you find in the following sentences:

(a) Selina will have her third one-man show next summer.

(b) The man complained bitterly to his neighbour's wife about the broken fence.

(c) The game-cocks fought hard, each one attacking his opponent more viciously than before.

(d) Each candidate had to write a description of himself/herself as he/she thought those who liked, and those who disliked, her/him would see her/him.

Jargon

Jargon is usually ugly-sounding and difficult to understand. It is the opposite of plain English. It involves the careless misuse or overuse of technical or semi-technical terms.

We read a lot of jargon every day in newspapers and hear it often in official pronouncements and public speaking. Here is an example given by Sir Ernest Gowers in *The Complete Plain Words* (p. 212):

Manpower ceilings are a very blunt macro-instrument and will be either ineffective or unduly restrictive if not based on the results of management reviews and other 'micro' activities . . . ceilings are biting, but this is what they were meant to do.

It is not possible to interpret exactly what the writer means, but the sentence could probably read:

An overall restriction on manpower should only be applied when all details of the situation have been fully considered. Restrictions will force changes, but this is what they were meant to do.

It may go unnoticed that words and phrases of jargon are cluttering sentences and obscuring meaning. Try to use technical words only when they express precisely what you want to say. Do not use them just because they come readily to mind; that is what turns them into jargon.

You may find Exercise 63 difficult, but this should help you to see why jargon should be avoided. If you are not able to rewrite the sentences in plain English, refer to the answers for help.

Exercise 64

Rewrite these sentences clearly, without the jargon.

(a)   The most efficient form of price control is a competitive situation where competitive pressures ensure the maximum productivity of factor inputs.

(b)   A grass-roots confrontation took place between the several representatives of the workers in the tool shop.

(c)   A meaningful discussion was held within the frame of reference suggested by the negotiator for the employees.

(d)   The depot is designed for integrated road and rail freight as a direct result of a developmental feasibility study.

(e)   A one-off meeting has been arranged between the two leaders.

(f)   They discussed a thought-provoking article which looked at the ongoing importance of European developments for British agriculture.

(g)   Annual repayments will be geared to the individual's cash flow.

(h)   A viable long-term structure needs to be taken into account when decisions are made about investment parameters.

(i)   The essential requirement for British agriculture is to be in a state of preparedness to respond to demand both in the UK and overseas and to make a maximum contribution to national wealth creation.

(j)   My profit-oriented views were not acceptable to the Board.

Technical language

Technical terms are often needed in order to express precisely what a 'specialist' writer has to convey to the reader. There's nothing wrong with using technical terms freely in their correct context. Here's an example of how an obscure piece of technical writing can be made simpler and clearer. This is the original:

> Undue attachment to the thesis that inflation is the result solely of institutional factors might cause the contribution made to inflation by excess demand to be neglected and the existence of excess demand to be prolonged.

Here is a better version:

> Inflation is caused not only by institutional factors but also by excess demand. Unless we recognize this and act on it, excess demand is likely to continue.

Think: Are you using technical language merely to impress your reader or perhaps because you cannot be bothered to think out something clearer? Advice given by Gowers in *The Complete Plain Words* is worth remembering: 'Be short, be simple, be human.' (p. 36, 2nd edn).

Exercise 65

Rewrite these sentences as simply as possible while retaining the original meaning. (My answers will naturally differ from yours.)

(a) By selecting extrapolations of current or emerging tendencies that grow continuously out of today's world, and reflect the multifold trend and our current expectations, we create a 'surprise-free' projection – one that seems less surprising than any other specific possibility.

(b) Although certain broad zonational patterns are discernible in the geographical distribution of animals as well as in those of soils and vegetation, the mobility of animals and, in the case of some, seasonal altitudinal migrations mean that the zonation becomes indistinct.

Clichés

It is when you are searching for a word or phrase to express an idea neatly and succinctly that you will be most tempted to use a cliché. Clichés are phrases, or sometimes single words, that have become worn out through overuse. The original user of the particular phrase may have said something illuminating and apt. Subsequent users 'borrow' the phrase on every possible occasion, and it becomes meaningless. Clichés are frequently found in everyday conversation and because of their familiarity you may use them in your writing without realizing that you are doing so.

For example, the sentence:

The motion was *well and truly* defeated when put to the vote.

could have been written:

The motion was easily defeated when put to the vote.

These sentences contain some typical clichés. Either write a better phrase to replace the cliché or rewrite the sentence completely, eliminating the cliché but retaining the original sense.

(a)   The Chancellor announced that as a result of the improved economic situation a wave of optimism was sweeping the country.

(b)   The spokeswoman made a public statement to the effect that the management's refusal to come to the bargaining table was the thin edge of the wedge.

(c)   It is a sad day for Britain when irresponsible wage awards to directors pave the way to rising inflation.

(d)   Time and again in this day and age we encounter examples of narrow specialism where problems have been solved in a limited context without a look at the wider consequences of the solutions or the ways and means used to achieve them.

(e)   We shall leave no stone unturned in our efforts to escape the tender mercies of those who are against us.

Metaphor

Metaphor is a way of making an idea or description vivid. It does this by a comparison or transfer of meaning from one thing to another. To be effective, a metaphor must be apt.

Try to pick out all the metaphors in this sentence:

The Government machine has become increasingly intricate, and Number Ten thus becomes the single ganglion of the nervous system, the apex of the pyramid, the only office which really knows everything that is going on.

It is obvious that the writer is trying to make a forceful point about how complex the workings of Government have become. Several metaphors are used, but these are quite unrelated to each other and evoke a series of confusing and rather ludicrous images in the reader's mind.

Extensive use of such metaphors often produces a ridiculous effect; for example:

The Rt Hon. Gentleman is leading the people over the precipice with his head in the sand.

Exercise 67

Here are some examples of mixed metaphors. For each example, write a couple of sentences pointing out the confusions.

(a) The wind of change is threatening to explode the stability of the currency system.

(b) Flexibility is one of the cornerstones of our new programme.

(c) Their political opponents had proffered the olive branch, but nothing concrete had come out of it.

(d) They will have to put their noses to the grindstone if they want to get this project off the ground.

Overused and abused terms

Look out for technical terms that are transferred incorrectly into
everyday speech and writing and for the many words in English that
have a precise meaning but which are used carelessly without regard to
their real meaning.

In this sentence the word 'crucial' is used correctly:

The meeting of the heads of departments to consider the proposed
degree courses will be the crucial one.

But here it is not:

A speedy end to widespread unemployment is crucial for our
economy.

'Crucial' means decisive or critical. It would have been better to write:

A speedy end to widespread unemployment is most important for
our economy.

If you are unsure about a word, check its meaning in your dictionary
and then look critically at the use to which it is put. You may find you
need your dictionary for the next exercise.

Exercise 68

Each pair of sentences provides a correct and an incorrect use of a
word. For each pair, tick the sentence which uses the word correctly and say what is wrong about its use in the incorrect sentence.

(a) (i) For an hour or two yesterday I had a really chronic
headache.

(ii) Through all those years he was always good-tempered
and serene, even though he was a chronic invalid.

(b) (i) I hate filling in forms; I must be allergic to them because
I always get something wrong in them.

(ii) After years of suffering from a hayfever-like irritation
he was found to be allergic to the fur of his own pet cat.

(c) (i) A generous donation from the company facilitated the
whole research project.

(ii) The research student was facilitated by an extremely
helpful archivist.

(d) (i) After the terrorist attack, they anticipated that new and
stricter security regulations would be imposed.

(ii) He saw that they had anticipated success by opening the
magnum of champagne before the results of the competition were
known.

Familiar but meaningless?

Think carefully about the use of very familiar words or phrases. The next exercise gives you more practice in noticing the incorrect use of familiar words. Some have no meaning at all in the sentence in which they are found.

Think: In your writing, do such words express what you want to say, or have they lost impact and become vague?

Exercise 69

Correct these sentences as necessary.

(a)   A man of his proportions would break such a flimsy chair.

(b)   I am in receipt of your letter of 4th inst. and will be replying as soon as I have any information for you.

(c)   The proceedings of the tribunal were held *in camera*.

(d)   There is every indication that the new corporation will be a tower of strength and forge ahead.

(e)   These investigations will be an essential input to the process of assessing market trends.

(f)   This document is forwarded herewith for the favour of your utilization.

(g)   The bankruptcy of Rolls-Royce produced a national trauma without real precedent.

A brief note on slang

Although slang is prevalent in everyday speech, it is rarely precise enough to be appropriate in essays and assignments. In writing, slang is found in journalism, particularly sporting journalism where it has become acceptable; but you are not likely to find slang acceptable to those who assess your written work.

6 *References and bibliographies*

References

References given in the body of an essay or report should state the sources of the information you have provided or of any passages you have quoted. A reference note must enable the reader to find a source as quickly and easily as possible.

Here is an example of a reference given at the end of a quoted passage:

Jennifer Uglow has observed that:

> George Eliot's art, like her life, shirks very little and questions much. She shows us a world where biological destiny, patriarchal law and ingrained social assumptions seem to combine in a web of constraint, where it may not be possible to reach all our goals, and where people are separated from each other and divided within themselves.
>
> Jennifer Uglow, *George Eliot* (Virago Press, 1987), p. 250

Subsequent references to the same source need not be given in full. The shortest comprehensible form of reference will be enough. For example, '*George Eliot*, p. 243' would constitute a satisfactory subsequent reference to the book cited in the above example.

References are sometimes given all together at the end of a book, sometimes at the end of each chapter, and sometimes as footnotes on the pages containing the matter they document.

The pattern of information given in a reference note is as follows:

(i)   author or editor's name as given on the title-page;
(ii) title (underlined or in italic);
(iii) publisher and date of publication (in parentheses);
(iv) page number(s).

Exercise 70

Write down very briefly what you think a bibliography is. To
check what you have written, look up the word 'bibliography' in
your dictionary. Check also in the Answers section of *Plain
English*. If necessary, correct or fill out your description.

The entries in a bibliography relate only to complete works, that is, to
whole books or articles. Most academic books have both a Bibliography and Reference Notes.

Describing a book for a bibliography

The main reason for including a book in a bibliography is to enable the
reader to locate the book, usually by going to a library. The information
in a bibliography should be sufficient to allow one to buy or to order the
book from a bookshop.

A basic bibliographic description of a book contains the following
three pieces of information:

(i) author's (or editor's) surname, followed by forename or initials;
(ii) title (underlined or in italics);
(iii) publisher and date of publication (in parentheses).

The detailed arrangement of these items of information may vary a
little, but the basic arrangement is like this:

Barber, D. (ed.), *Farming and Wildlife* (Royal Society for the
Protection of Birds, 1970)

Gaskell, P., *A New Introduction to Bibliography* (Clarendon
Press, 1972)

Hardyment, Christina, *From Mangle to Microwave* (Polity, 1990)

Notice that the entries are in alphabetical order, and that the first
word and all the main words in the book's title begin with a capital
letter. Notice also that titles of books are *printed in italics*. In writing
they should be underlined, because underlining something in writing
means exactly the same as printing it in italics. The way to indicate to a
printer that you want something printed in italics is to underline it in the
typescript. No full stop is needed (optional) at the end of a bibliographic entry.

If you have a book that you want to describe for a bibliography, where do you find the essential bits of information?

The title, the name of the author or editor, and the publisher's name appear on the title-page. The year of publication may also appear on the title-page; otherwise you will find it on the back of the title-page. Many books have a page before the title-page called the 'half-title'. The information contained on the half-title varies, and the only constant feature is probably the book's title.

Exercise 72

Now take three of your own books and write their descriptions as for a bibliography.

(a)

(b)

(c)

If you had any difficulty fitting any of your descriptions to the basic form I have outlined, you might like to turn to 'Additional information', on p. 97, where complications such as editions and translations are dealt with.

Useful abbreviations for bibliographies and references

Before going on to the description of papers and articles for a bibliography, you will need to know a few of the common abbreviations frequently used in bibliographies and references. I shall simply list them here, and you can practise using them in later exercises.

ch.(chs.)	chapter(s)
ed.(eds.)	editor(s); edited by
edn	edition
eq.	equation
et al.	(Latin, = *et alii*) and others; used when there are more than two authors or editors it should be underlined or written in italics
fig.(figs.)	figure(n)
fn.	footnote
l., ll.	line, lines
no.(nos.)	number(s)
p., pp.	page, pages
rev.	revised (by)
tr.	translator; translated (by)
vol.(vols.)	volume(s)

Describing papers and articles for a bibliography

Papers or articles published in a book

The basic description carries the following information:

(i) author's surname, followed by forename or initials;

(ii) title of the paper or article, in single quotation marks:

(iii) details of the book as described above: editor's name, title of book (underlined or italic), publisher and date of publication in parentheses;

(iv) page numbers of the first and last pages of the paper or article.

Again, the details may vary slightly. Here are two examples of the basic arrangement:

Page, R. W., 'Population Forecasting', in H. S. D. Cole *et al.* (eds), *Thinking about the Future* (Chatto & Windus/Sussex University Press, 1973), pp. 159–74

Rogers, Michael, 'Computers and Language: An Optimistic View', in Christopher Ricks and Leonard Michaels (eds), *The State of the Language* (Faber and Faber, 1990), pp. 195–299

Papers or articles published in journals or periodicals

Journals and periodicals are usually published at regular intervals over a period of many years. They are often bound up in volumes for keeping in libraries. Full details are therefore needed if an article is to be found easily. The basic description requires the following information:

(i) author's surname, followed by forename or initials;
(ii) title of the paper or article, in single quotation marks (note that titles of papers and articles are not fully capitalized);
(iii) title of the journal or periodical, underlined or italic and with capital first letters of main words;
(iv) volume number;
(v) issue number (not all journals have these);
(vi) date of issue (in parentheses);
(vii) page numbers of the first and last pages of the paper or article.

The details of the date depend on the frequency with which the journal is published. The year of publication is essential. For a quarterly or monthly journal, the season or month of issue is useful, but not essential if the issue number is given. For a weekly publication (e.g. *New Scientist* or *Nature*), the full date of issue is of more use than the issue number. Note that it is usual to use a lower-case 't' for the word 'the' when referring to the *Independent*, the *Poetry Review*, the *Guardian*, and so on. Exceptions to this convention are *The Times* and *The Economist*.

Here are two examples:

Rose-Innes, A. C., 'The new superconductors', *Contemporary Physics*, vol. 7, no. 2 (1965), pp. 135–51

Stansell, J., 'North Sea gas – an ever changing pipedream', *New Scientist*, vol. 79, no. 1113 (27 July 1978), pp. 264–5

There is a point to note about page numbers. These should be given with the minimum number of figures consistent with the pronunciation. You will see that in the examples I have written '135–51', '264–5', '100–4' and '50–1', in each case not repeating the figures that remain the same. On the other hand, we must write '13–17' or '215–19', because of the way in which they are read aloud.

Exercise 73

Write descriptions for a bibliography of the following articles:

(a)   There is a good review article by Bernard Lovell called 'Into the cosmic depths'. It is on page 7 of *The Times Literary Supplement* for 9 August 1991, issue number 4610.

(b)   D. Nicholls wrote a review article called 'Theories of acids and bases', which was published in the journal *Chemistry Student* in 1967. It runs from p. 33 to p. 38 of issue no. 2 of volume 1 of the journal. The same article was subsequently reprinted on pp. 191–204 of a book called *Modern Chemistry* edited by J. G. Stark and published by Penguin in 1970. (Write two separate descriptions.)

Additional information

Many books that continue in print for a number of years are periodically revised and brought out in a new edition. When listing such a book in a bibliography, it is important to make sure that your reader can find the exact edition that you have used. You will often find the edition number printed on the cover of a book, but the best place to look is on the back of the title-page, where the book's publishing history is given. Ignore all the reprintings that are not given new edition numbers and find the latest edition number and the corresponding date; that is, the edition you are handling. Here are just two examples:

Gordon, J. E., *The New Science of Strong Materials*, 2nd edn (Penguin, 1976)

Mason, B., *Principles of Geochemistry*, 3rd edn (Wiley, 1966)

You may occasionally find yourself reading a translation. Here is just one example:

Born, M., *The Restless Universe*, 2nd edn, tr. W. M. Deans (Dover, 1951)

Convert the following information into a bibliography, arranging the entries in alphabetical order of first author's (editor's) names.

(a)   There is a book by Robert A. Solo that you will need. It was published by Macmillan of New York in 1991 and is called *The Philosophy of Science and Economics*.

(b)   Recently my wife bought me an early copy of the Pelican *Metals in the Service of Man* by William Alexander and Arthur Street from our local Oxfam shop; it is the third edition, published by Penguin in 1946.

(c)   In volume 10, issue no. 3 of *Contemporary Physics*, published in 1969, there is an article called 'Electrolysis and simple cells' by R. Parsons on pp. 205–20.

(d)   I am keen to get hold of a book by Ahmad Y. Al Hassan and Donald R. Hill, published in 1991 by the Cambridge University Press under the title *Islamic Technology: an Illustrated History*.

Answers to the exercises

Punctuation

Exercise 1

Brunel's critics still refused to be convinced and now maintained that when the time came to remove the centering altogether the bridge would surely collapse. The engineer himself had no doubts whatever about his bridge but he ruled that the centres should not be removed finally until it had stood through another winter. The suspicion that this was due not so much to excessive caution as to an impish sense of humour is hard to resist. Certainly the fact that the bridge was standing entirely free for nine months while his jealous opponents supposed that the centering was still helping to support it was a joke that Brunel must have relished keenly. Its point was revealed and his critics confounded by a violent storm one autumn night in 1839 which blew all the useless centering down.

L. T. C. Rolt, *Isambard Kingdom Brunel* (Penguin, 1970), p. 172

Exercise 2

For each sentence, answer (i) indicates the least number of full stops that is consistent with good modern practice; answer (ii) is an equally acceptable version with all the possible full stops added.

(a)   (i) Mr and Mrs J. B. Jones, who live at 23 St James's Gardens, told PC Alderbank that they had been woken at 3 a.m. by the sound of glass breaking and had seen a man running out of the house opposite, no. 26.
(ii) Mr. and Mrs. J. B. Jones, who live at 23 St. James's Gardens, told P.C. Alderbank that they had been woken at 3 a.m. by the sound of glass breaking and had seen a man running out of the house opposite, no. 26.

(b)   (i) The TV programme I liked so much was on either BBC 1 or BBC 2 and was presented by a Dr T. W. Fox.
(ii) The T.V. programme I liked so much was on either B.B.C. 1 or B.B.C. 2 and was presented by a Dr. T. W. Fox.

(c) (i) In March 1979 the Royal Society held a discussion meeting on nuclear magnetic resonance (n.m.r.) of intact biological systems organized by Prof. R. J. P. Williams, FRS, Prof. E. R. Andrew and Dr G. K. Radda.

(ii) In March 1979 the Royal Society held a discussion meeting on nuclear magnetic resonance (n.m.r.) of intact biological systems organized by Prof. R. J. P. Williams, F.R.S., Prof. E. R. Andrew and Dr. G. K. Radda.

Exercise 3

Within the wider community of British universities the Open University is the only one which as a general rule demands no entrance qualifications of its students. This means that foundation courses play a vital role in its teaching system. They form the bridge between students of enormously varied educational backgrounds and the higher-level courses that will enable them to become graduates.

Exercise 4

The Castner cell underwent various slight modifications during the first quarter of the century, but in 1924 the American J. C. Downs patented a cell for the production of sodium from fused sodium chloride. This consisted of a steel tank lined with firebrick containing a massive cylindrical graphite anode projecting through the base, surrounded coaxially by a cathode of iron gauze. By adding calcium chloride to the sodium chloride, the melting-point of the electrolyte is reduced from 800 °C to 505 °C. The energy efficiency of the Downs cell process from salt to sodium is about three times greater than that of the composite process of first producing sodium hydroxide in a mercury cell, followed by further electrolysis in a Castner cell. However, both processes were in operation in 1950. The price of sodium in the U.S.A. dropped from $2.00 per pound in 1890 to $0.15 per pound in 1946.

T. I. Williams, ed., *A History of Technology*, vol. 6
(Oxford University Press, 1978), pp. 519–21

Do not worry if you were not aware that Castner is a personal name. Note that the full stops in U.S.A. are optional; USA is equally correct. Also note that 'Downs-cell' instead of 'Downs cell' is entirely acceptable.

Exercise 5

(a) Your home may be heated by solid fuel, oil, gas or electricity. (*Alternatively:* . . . solid fuel, oil, gas, or electricity.)

(b)   Resources are defined as energy, materials, labour and capital.
(*Or:* . . . labour, and capital.)

(c)   He found he needed several metres of electric cable, three junction boxes, a packet of insulated staples, four light-switches and an assortment of tools.
(*Or:* . . . four light-switches, and an assortment of tools.)

Exercise 6

(a)   Copper is a malleable, ductile metal.

(b)   Many new electronic gadgets have appeared in recent years.

(c)   The new crystals tended to be long, smooth, whip-like filaments.

Exercise 7

(a)   The engine stalled, the brakes failed and the car started to roll backwards.

(b)   Britain now has a system as advanced as any in the world, and other countries are adopting similar systems.

(c)   I was finding it hard to keep up with the course and had missed one or two lectures, but I made a point of going to all the tutorials and handing in my essays on time.

(d)   Seaside habitats are equally rich and provide great contrasts in species.

Exercise 8

(a)   All matter is made up of atoms, and all atoms are made up of an inner nucleus (plural: nuclei) surrounded by electrons. Almost the whole mass of the atom is concentrated in the nucleus, but the nucleus is much smaller than the whole atom. The bulk of the nucleus is made up of protons and neutrons. All the atoms of a particular chemical element contain the same number of protons, and this number is known as the atomic number of the element. The atomic number of hydrogen is 1, that of carbon is 6 and that of oxygen is 8. This means that all hydrogen atoms contain 1 proton, all carbon atoms contain 6 protons and all oxygen atoms contain 8 protons.

(b)   The pressure, volume and temperature of a fixed quantity of gas are interrelated. Boyle's law states that at constant temperature the volume of a given mass of gas is inversely proportional to the pressure, and Charles's law states that at constant pressure the volume of a given mass of gas is directly proportional to the absolute temperature. For a mole of gas these two laws may be combined in the gas equation $pV = RT$. In this equation p is the pressure, V is the volume, R is the gas constant and T is the absolute temperature. Gases do not strictly obey the gas laws, but follow them more and more closely as the pressure of the gas is reduced.

Exercise 9

(a)   Heavy chemicals are essentially those produced in bulk and used in large quantities; fine chemicals are made on a comparatively small scale, some indeed in quantities of only a pound or two.

T. I. Williams, The Chemical Industry (Penguin, 1953), p. 120

(b)   However, technology does not make the only claim on manpower; planning, to be mentioned in a moment, also requires a comparatively high level of specialized talent.

J. K. Galbraith, The New Industrial State, 2nd edn
(Deutsch, 1972), p. 15; (Penguin edn, 1974), p. 34

(c)   Fox Talbot's sensitive material, like Daguerre's, was silver iodide, formed not more than a day before use as a thin film on paper which was brushed successively with solutions of silver nitrate and potassium iodide; the sensitivity to light was increased by further treatment with gallic acid, the sensitizing properties of this having been discovered in 1837 by J. B. Reade, another British pioneer.

T. K. Derry and T. I. Williams, A Short History of Technology,
paperback edn (Oxford University Press, 1970), p. 655

Exercise 10

Although this branch of the chemical industry is the one with which the general public most frequently comes into direct contact it is nevertheless one about which many misconceptions exist. Plastics are often spoken of as though there was little difference between the various kinds; in fact they differ enormously in their properties. Plastics are often thought of as new substances; in fact they have been in use for a century. Plastics are often regarded as cheap substitutes for other and better constructional materials such as wood, metal, and natural textiles; in fact many have found favour on their own merits and often are far from cheap.

The Chemical Industry, p. 173

You may, of course, omit the comma after 'metal' in the last sentence.

Exercise 11

(a)   The steelworkers' representative, a foundryman from Humberside, argued for rapid modernization.

102

(b) It was his spelling, not his punctuation, that he needed to improve.

(c) He had, no doubt, a speech carefully prepared for the occasion.

(d) There are two alternatives for punctuating this sentence, depending on the way 'however' is being used:

(i) These incidents, however trivial in themselves, are liable to lead to more serious demonstrations.

Or, depending on meaning:

(ii) However, these incidents, trivial in themselves, are liable to lead to more serious demonstrations.

Exercise 12

(a) The fire having been lit for some time, the room was quite warm.

(b) The fire, having been lit for some time, needed stoking.

(c) Obtaining planning permission for this factory will not be easy.
Or Obtaining planning permission, for this factory, will not be easy. [The addition of the commas emphasizes the difficulty in the case of this particular factory.]

(d) The results of his early experiments being positive, he was encouraged to embark on a more ambitious programme of research.

(e) The charge on the anode, being positive, attracts the negatively charged anions.

Exercise 13

Tyres, of course, have the function of spreading and cushioning the load beneath the wheels of a vehicle, and in this they are extremely successful. However, tyres are really only one example of a whole class of blown-up structures. Quite apart from any cushioning effects, blown-up structures provide a very effective way of evading the serious penalties in weight and cost which are incurred when we try to carry light loads over a long distance in bending or in compression.

J. E. Gordon, *Structures* (Penguin, 1978), pp. 314–15

Exercise 14

(a) Four types of malt whisky are made in Scotland: Campbeltown, Highland, Islay and Lowland.
(*Or:* . . . Islay, and Lowland.)

(b) Time is short: sixteen months is all we have.

(c)   Charles Darwin wrote: 'I am convinced that Natural Selection has been the main but not exclusive means of modification.'

Exercise 15

Chapman develops three basic scenarios for future patterns of fuel demand in Britain: 'business-as usual', 'technical-fix', and 'low-growth' scenarios. These represent, respectively: the virtually unrestrained projection of present trends, the introduction of some technical changes to effect a more moderate growth in fuel demand, and more radical proposals to effect a very definite restriction in the growth of fuel demand and aimed eventually at stabilizing demand. For each case, Chapman explores how the various components of total fuel demand would change, and the policy options that would need to be exercised to supply the various demands. This exploration is succinctly conveyed, but rests on considerable analysis and Chapman's specialist knowledge of energy demands and the fuel industries.

> The Open University, T361 *Control of Technology*, Unit 8
> (Open University, 1978), p. 14

Exercise 16

(a)   If you are not confident about your spelling, turn to the next section of this book, where you will find some useful spelling tests and exercises.

(b)   When you have studied energy in more detail, as you will do later in this course, you will realize how often in everyday life we use energy-conversion devices, of which the electric kettle is a familiar example.

Exercise 17

(a)   Describing: 'who by now was only a few yards off'.
Defining: 'whom I had seen that morning at the inn'.

(c)   Defining: 'where I was born'.

(c)   Defining: 'when beer was twopence a pint'.

(d)   Describing: 'where we are opening a new factory'.

Exercise 18

(a)   People who live in country districts are particularly affected by the withdrawal of bus services.
Defining: 'who live in country districts'.

(b) I want you to know the basic rules which govern punctuation.
Defining: 'which govern punctuation'.

(c) The book, which I think you should read gives a full account of nuclear power.
Defining: 'which I think you should read'.

(d) It was a letter from my mother, who was worried because I had not written lately.
Describing: 'who was worried because I had not written lately'. (I do not need to define my mother.)

(e) Usually my brother met me at the station, but on that memorable Friday it was my father who came to meet me.
Defining: 'who came to meet me'.

How can this be a defining clause? I do not have several fathers, of whom this is one. The key to the riddle lies in the word 'it'. In (d) you will see immediately that 'it' is 'a letter', but in (e) 'it' does not seem to be anything at all. What the sentence really means is something like: 'Usually my brother met me at the station, but on that memorable Friday the person who came to meet me was my father.' So the person that 'who came to meet me' defines is not actually in the sentence.

I put this exercise in to make the point that, although I have tried to present you with simple rules to help you with your punctuation and have tried to choose examples and exercises to exemplify these rules, the English language refuses to be bound by simple rules. The guidance I can offer you is therefore bound to be limited.

Exercise 19

Although bats flourish and survive very well today, pterodactyls were superseded by birds, which have feathers, a great many years ago. It is possible, of course, that the extinction of pterodactyls had nothing to do with structural considerations, but it is also possible that there is something special about feathers which gives birds an edge over other flying creatures. When I worked at the Royal Aircraft Establishment I used to ask my superiors, from time to time, whether it would not perhaps be better if aeroplanes had feathers; but I seldom succeeded in extracting a rational or even a patient answer to this question.

Exercise 20

(a) the amplifier's gain
(b) the amplifiers' gains
(c) chemistry's importance
(d) the gas's properties
(e) the gases' properties
(f) the men's occupations

Exercise 21

(a) Its roof was insulated.
(b) It's too early for the pubs to be open.
(c) I must have overloaded its circuits.
(d) Its main disadvantage is its weight.
(e) It's the latest model and its performance is second to none.
(f) It's not easy to understand relativity theory because its concepts are mathematical.

Exercise 22

Why have I called the package a 'unit'? Because it represents a week's worth of your time: one week of student study is the basic unit of the Open University's arithmetic course. The remainder of this course is built around a set of 'blocks', each of which contains several units' worth of work. Studying each unit will involve not just reading text, but also watching television, listening to radio, working with audiovision and writing assignments.

Exercise 23

'Polychlorinated biphenyls (PCBs) should be regarded as if they were carcinogenic to humans,' says a report by the International Agency for Research on Cancer (*IARC Monographs*, vol. 18). But the authoritative and cautious IARC says there is insufficient evidence to decide whether polybrominated biphenyls (PBBs), the close chemical cousins of PCBs, are also carcinogenic.

New Scientist (11 January 1979), p. 78

Exercise 24

Figure 16 shows the pattern of energy flow in the United Kingdom. In 1975 gross consumption of *primary energy* in the United Kingdom was approximately 2425 TW h (1TW h $=$ 10^9kW h). But, because of inefficiencies in energy conversion and distribution, some 30 per cent or so (725 TW h) is lost between producer and consumer. Even when this *delivered energy* finally arrives at the point of consumption, further losses of around 30 per cent (725 TW h) occur in the appliances and processes in which it is used. Central-heating boilers, for instance, have efficiencies of only 60 per cent or so, open coal fires are even worse, with a typical efficiency of only 20 per cent, and motor cars with internal combustion engines are still less efficient (less than 20 per cent).

The Open University, T361 *Control of Technology*, Units 10–11
(Open University, 1978), p. 68

Exercise 25

(a)   The start of the second phase of the three-year programme was set back a month.

(b)   This will be a set-back for your far-fetched schemes; perhaps it will bring you down to earth.

(c)   This recently published report contains up-to-date information on low-level radiation leaks from advanced gas-cooled reactors.

Exercise 26

On the other hand, the *unit* costs (or 'run-on costs') of printing the magazine on a hand-operated duplicating machine will be relatively high, for various reasons:

(a)   The machine, because it is hand operated, can produce relatively few copies per hour, so the labour cost of each copy is relatively high.

(b)   The machine, for technical reasons, has to use fairly heavy paper, which makes the cost of each copy relatively high. Also the stencil, being made of waxed paper, will break up after, say, a thousand copies or so, and a new one will have to be typed.

(c)   The machine prints only one page at a time, so that when all the sheets (thirty-two of them for a sixty-four-page magazine) are finally printed it takes a long time to collate them by hand and staple them into a magazine.

T361 Control of Technology, Units 10–11, p. 53

Exercise 27

(a)   (i) No one has yet built a living organism (however simple) starting from scratch.
(ii) No one has yet built a living organism, however simple, starting from scratch.

Commas give the best effect here.

(b)   (i) A combination of three types of study (two on humans and one on animals) indicates strongly that alcohol is harmful to unborn babies.
(ii) A combination of three types of study, two on humans and one on animals, indicates strongly that alcohol is harmful to unborn babies.

Perhaps the case for parentheses is stronger than for (a), but I still prefer the commas.

Exercise 28

(a) The Chinese are thrifty people: the excavated earth was used to make bricks for the tunnel walls.

(b) Already it has sold six systems: three in Denmark, two in Spain and one in Italy.

In both these examples I prefer the colon.

Exercise 29

This is how I would punctuate the passage:

> A purely inorganic compound with optical activity, the first for almost 50 years, has just been synthesized by Robert Gillard and Franz Winmer of University College, Cardiff. Most known optically active compounds – molecules with structures that cannot be superimposed upon their mirror image – contain carbon atoms. They are either organic compounds or chelates, i.e. complexes of transition metals where the carbon atoms help form the claw-like ligands.

The pair of dashes that I have retained mark off the explanation of the term 'optically active compounds' that is inserted in the middle of sentence. If such an explanation occurred at the end of a sentence it could be introduced by a colon, but this cannot be done in the middle of a sentence because there is no suitable punctuation mark to end such an explanation. This is where dashes are most useful.

You may think I cheated by inserting an 'i.e.' in place of the last dash. I do not think a colon will do here because the words after the dash (in the original) define only the word 'chelates'. Another solution is to put the definition in brackets.

You will see I also omitted the comma before 'or'. A comma is not required in a simple 'either . . . or . . .' phrase like this.

Exercise 30

(a) It is found that meteors fall into two distinct classes: the stony and the iron–nickel types, with a few intermediate or stony–iron types.

E. F. Slade, *Interfaces of Physics* (Penguin, 1973), p. 130

(b) The Beer–Lambert law is an extension of a law proposed by Lambert in 1760, which stated that layers of equal thickness of a homogeneous material absorb equal proportions of light.

(c) Einstein suggested that the path of a particle in four-dimensional space–time is a geodesic.

Spelling

Exercise 31

(a) beginning
(b) allotted
(c) benefited
(d) compelling

Exercise 32

(a) wrong   successful
(b) right
(c) wrong   occasionally
(d) wrong   committee
(e) wrong   exaggerate
(f) wrong   abbreviate
(g) wrong   parallel
(h) wrong   omission
(i) right
(j) right

Exercise 33

(a) achieved
(b) quotient
(c) deficient
(d) ceiling
(e) perceive

Exercise 34

(a) right
(b) wrong   accelerator
(c) right
(d) wrong   inventor
(e) wrong   distributor
(f) right

Exercise 35

(a) substances
(b) recurrence
(c) inferences
(d) resistance
(e) performance

Exercise 36

(a) homogeneous
(b) nutritious
(c) precarious
(d) meticulous
(e) numerous
(f) erroneous
(g) cautious
(h) enormous

Exercise 37

(a) agreeable
(b) illegible
(c) visible
(d) durable
(e) flexible
(f) adjustable

(a) binary
(b) machinery
(c) necessary
(d) contemporary

(e) periphery
(f) delivery
(g) primary

Exercise 39

(a) extension
(b) distribution
(c) repulsion

(d) transmission
(e) restriction
(f) construction

Exercise 40

(a) proceed
(b) supersede

(c) precede
(d) succeed

Exercise 41

(a) ascertain
(b) miscellaneous
(c) conscious
(d) discipline

(e) artificial
(f) official
(g) essential
(h) initial

Grammar

Exercise 42

(a) Non-sentence
Force and inertia are related concepts in physics.

(b) Non-sentence
Worms and insects live in the soil.

(c) Sentence
Subject: John Stuart Mill
Verb: realized

(d) Sentence
Subject: it
Verb: follows

(e) Non-sentence
There is a natural cycle for every element needed for life, each with its own natural circulation rate.

(f)   Non-sentence
Pollution may result from getting rid of wastes at the least possible cost.

(g)   Sentence
Subject: Gaseous emissions
Verb: may become

(h)   Non-sentence
A way was found of generating electric currents from mechanical motion and hence of converting mechanical energy to electrical.

(i)   Sentence
Subject: The rate
Verb: has been determined

(j)   Non-sentence
In the process of cracking, large molecules are broken down into smaller ones by means of high temperatures and pressures.

(k)   Non-sentence
Intensification of farming leads to soil deterioration and eventually erosion.

(l)   Sentence
Subject: it
Verb: seems

Exercise 43

(a)   'Consists in' should be 'consists of'.
(b)   'Than my calculator batteries,' should be 'when my calculator batteries'.
(c)   Will you join me for a pint?
(d)   'Protest at' should be 'protest against'.
(e)   'Judged on' should be either 'judged by' or preferably 'judged according to'.

Exercise 44

(a)   He is afraid of George and *me*.
(b)   Correct
(c)   He gave it to both me and *him*.
(d)   Between you and *me*, he probably won't come.
(e)   Correct.

Exercise 45

(a)   The amount of viscosity exhibited by different fluids *varies*.

(b)   So much water and oil *have* been drawn from underground that the resources are much depleted.

(c)   A library of subroutines *contributes* to the value of a computer installation in much the same way as an extra piece of equipment would do.

(d)   The limitation of exhaust emissions and atmospheric pollution generally by the application of smoke-control regulations *is* a further step in the improvement of the road-user's environment.

(e)   This sentence is correct.

Exercise 46

(a)   'ever' is unnecessary.

(b)   'of' is unnecessary.

(c)   'Being' is unnecessary.

(d)   'about' is unnecessary.

(e)   'up' is unnecessary.

Exercise 47

(a)   This sentence is difficult to rearrange, and a better solution is to replace 'what' with 'why': Why have you given it to me?

(b)   I was envious of their new house.
Although this is a solution, some of the emphasis of the original is lost. Another possibility is: It was their new house that I envied.

(c)   The 'to' is unnecessary.
When I began the journey, I was unsure where I was going.

Exercise 48

(a)   affected

(b)   affect

(c)   effect

(d)   effected

Exercise 49

In (a) the quiet running will be influenced (perhaps to be less quiet, perhaps to be more) by the adjustment. In (b) quiet running will result from the adjustment.

Exercise 50

(a)   The bar graph is used to represent data that *are* either nominally or ordinally scaled.

(b)   It is easy to work out the circumference of a circle once the length of a *radius* is known.

(c) If neither of these experimental methods *is* successful you must try a third one.

(d) The committee *were* divided in their opinions.

(e) In your essays you may write 'none is' or 'none are'; either *is* acceptable.

(f) Adding the *indices* is a method of multiplication used in mathematics.

(g) Each of the units of measurement *was* originally *a* natural *unit* based on the *length* of *a* certain *part* of the human hand or foot.
Or
All the units of measurement were originally natural units based on the lengths of certain parts of the human hand or foot.

(h) The action of *bacteria breaks* down the carbon compounds of plant systems to carbon dioxide and water.

(i) In a White Paper of 1970 a network of motorways for England of 4200 miles *was* proposed.

(j) What is your *criterion* for making such a judgement?
Or
What *are* your criteria for making such a judgement?

(k) This sentence is correct.

(l) *Both* distribution through microwave radio links using tall towers *and* transmission from a satellite far above the surface of the earth are possible ways of disseminating television.
Or
Either distribution through microwave radio links using tall towers or transmission from a satellite far above the surface of the earth *is a* possible *way* of disseminating television.

Exercise 51

(a)	practice	(h)	principle
(b)	principal	(i)	compliment
(c)	practised	(j)	defuse
(d)	complement	(k)	stationery
(e)	diffuse	(l)	stationary
(f)	discreet	(m)	proceeded
(g)	precedes	(n)	discrete

Exercise 52

(a) Only I spoke to my tutor yesterday.
Meaning: I was the one person who spoke to my tutor yesterday.

(b)   I only spoke to my tutor yesterday.
Meaning: I did not see my tutor, I spoke to him yesterday.

(c)   I spoke only to my tutor yesterday.
Meaning: I spoke to my tutor yesterday, but not to anyone else.

(d)   I spoke to my only tutor yesterday.
Meaning: I have just one tutor, to whom I spoke yesterday.

(e)   I spoke to my tutor only yesterday.
Meaning: I spoke to my tutor as recently as yesterday.

(f)   I spoke to my tutor yesterday only.
Meaning: The one day on which I spoke to my tutor was yesterday.

Note   You may have felt the meanings indicated above are different from the ones you have given. The intonation, or speed and stress, in reading the sentences may alter the interpretation; versions besides those given may be correct. The important thing is to realize how much the sense may be altered by small rearrangements of words in a sentence.

Exercise 53

(a)   Although the shark-spotting helicopter was circling over the -bathers, it apparently failed to see the shark.

(b)   This sentence is confusing and subject to many interpretations; here is one:
As the guard went about his duties, the man watched him closely, noting the time he came to feed the prisoner.

(c)   Again this is open to various interpretations:
I told my mother that she should help the woman.

(d)   If the baby doesn't thrive on raw milk, boil the milk.

(e)   In my desk there are some sticking plasters which I keep for emergencies.

Exercise 54

(a)   fewer
(b)   comprised
(c)   lay

Exercise 55

(a)   Correct. Rule 3, therefore *whom*: to (preposition) whom.

(b)   Incorrect. Rule 3, therefore *whom*: from (preposition) whom.

114

(c)   Incorrect. Rule 1, therefore *who*: who is illiterate. 'It appears' is, as it were, in brackets.

(d)   Correct. Rule 2, therefore *whom*: we thought whom (object) to be trustworthy.

(e)   Incorrect. Rule 1, therefore *who*: who is coming to tea? 'Do you suppose' is, as it were, in brackets.

Exercise 56

(a)   specific variations in the design of a system that uses diesel fuel
Or
variations in the design of a specific system that uses diesel fuel

(b)   *Possibly*: a comprehensive network(?) for the exchange of information

(c)   a programme for the improvement of domestic accommodation [i.e. housing]

Exercise 57

(a)   We thank you for your order and, being always anxious to carry out our customers' wishes immediately, *we ask if you would* kindly state the address to which you wish the goods to be delivered.

(b)   Whilst requesting you to furnish the return now outstanding *we advise you* that in future no further credit will be extended.

(c)   *It was* administered at first by the National Gallery; *in* 1917 the appointment of a separate board and director enabled a fully independent policy to be pursued.

(d)   Arising out of a confrontation between the Government and the Opposition over devolution, *an early vote of no confidence in the Government may be sought by the Opposition.*

Exercise 58

(a)   It is difficult with this example because 'scarcely' should have been matched with the positive verb 'was'. Logically interpreted it would be: *He was quite able* to read the book.

(b)   '*I did say something*,' she protested.

(c)   This suggests that the solution could be worked with difficulty: It's *just about a workable* solution.

(d)   This implies that there was some compulsion to go; it was not possible to refuse. Perhaps it is best rewritten as: I *was obliged to go.*

(e)   *Everyone* in this room *has* sometimes lied.

Exercise 59

(a) It is the intention of the Minister of Transport to increase substantially all present rates by means of a general percentage.

(b) We intend to support further attempts at obtaining a truce.
Or
We intend to continue to support attempts at obtaining a truce.

Note Although the sentence, 'We intend to support further attempts at obtaining a truce' is grammatically correct, its meaning is not clear. In this version 'further' could apply to either 'support' or to 'attempts'; from the sentence given originally we know that it relates to 'support'.

(c) He still seems to be allowed to speak at demonstrations.

(d) The greatest difficulty about assessing the economic achievements of the Government is that its spokespersons always tend to exaggerate them.

(e) The directors are said strongly to favour these reforms.

(f) It will be possible to improve considerably our working conditions.

Style

Exercise 60

(a) I was late with my work because I found the calculations difficult, and so I didn't know whether my tutor would mark it.

(b) The Prime Minister went on to say that it was hoped that everyone would support the new environmental measures. Backbenchers gave the scheme their unqualified support.

(c) If there is anything more I can do in the next few weeks to further the project, I will do it.

Exercise 61

(a) etc.
(b) i.e.
(c) i.e.
(d) e.g.
(e) i.e.

Exercise 62

(a) Omit *to try*; it is contained in *attempt*.
(b) Change to: The mortar *may* crack.
(c) Omit *in the past*.

(d)   Omit *in shape*; it is implied in *square*.

(e)   Omit *about*, or omit *The subject of*.

(f)   Change *because* to *that*.

Exercise 63

(a)   Selina will have her third solo show next summer.

(b)   The man complained bitterly to his neighbour (or . . . to the woman next door) about the broken fence.

(c)   This sentence is correct: it is not necessary to change 'his' to 'its' since game-cocks are, by definition, male.

(d)   The candidates had to write descriptions of themselves as they thought those who liked, and those who disliked, them would see them.

Exercise 64

(a)   Competition encourages cheap production and so helps to control prices.

(b)   The representatives of the tool-shop workers disagreed strongly.

(c)   There was a useful discussion of the matters presented by the employees' negotiator.

(d)   As a result of careful investigation, the depot has been designed to take both road and rail freight.

(e)   The two leaders will meet once.

(f)   They discussed an article which examined the importance of European developments for British agriculture.

(g)   Each borrower will make yearly repayments that relate to his or her other income.

(h)   When investing money one must consider the future.

(i)   British agriculture must be ready to respond to home and overseas demand and to help improve the national income.

(j)   My views on profit differed from those of the Board.

Exercise 65

(a)   By looking at current trends we can estimate likely future developments.

(b)   Animals, plants and soils are distributed in zones; because of the mobility of animals, and the seasonal migrations of some, the boundaries of their zones are the least distinct.

Exercise 66

(a)   The Chancellor announced that the country was becoming more optimistic as a result of the stronger economy.

(b)   The spokeswoman stated publicly that the management's refusal to negotiate was only the beginning of the matter.

(c)   Britain faces rising inflation when directors receive excessive salary increases.

(d)   We often encounter examples of narrow specialism, where problems have been solved in a limited context without regard to the wider consequences of the solutions and to the means that achieved them.

(e)   We shall do everything possible to remain unaffected by our opponents.

Exercise 67

(a)   Winds do not explode; they may destroy or devastate. 'Wind' does not make clear what is happening to the currency.

(b)   It is not reassuring to have to think of flexibility as a property of a cornerstone.

(c)   It's difficult to think of something concrete coming out of an olive branch, so this mixed metaphor adds nothing to our understanding.

(d)   This mix of metaphors evokes a ludicrous mental image and so fails to make the serious point that is intended.

Exercise 68

(a)   Sentence (ii) is correct.
A chronic illness is one that is long-lasting. In (i), therefore, 'severe' would be a better word to use.

(b)   Sentence (ii) is correct.
'Allergic' is a medical term which describes the condition of a patient who is sensitive to some substance that is normally harmless. It could be allowed that in (i) it is a metaphorical description of a possible reaction to filling in forms.

(c)   Sentence (i) is correct.
'Facilitate' means to make easy or help forward. In (ii) it is used as if it meant 'given the services of' or 'assisted by'. It was the research that was facilitated, not the student.

(d)   Sentence (ii) is correct.
To anticipate something is to act as if it is already the case. It does not mean the same as 'to expect'.

Exercise 69

(a)   A man of his weight would break such a flimsy chair.
('Of his proportions' is a cliché; the word 'weight' is simpler and clearer to the reader.)

(b)   I have received your letter of the 4th and will be replying as soon as I have any information for you.
('Am in receipt of your letter of 4th inst.' is an example of office jargon; the revised version is a more natural way of expressing the sense of the original phrase.)

(c)   This sentence is correct; '*in camera*' is used in its specific sense of 'not held in public'.

(d)   There is every indication that the new corporation will be very successful. ('Tower of strength' and 'forge ahead' form a mixed metaphor. They merely confuse the reader: the one suggests immobility, the other movement.)

(e)   These investigations will make an important contribution to the assessment of market trends.
('Input' is a sloppy use of a technical term from computer language.)

(f)   Please use this form.
(This is probably what the writer meant in plain English.)

(g)   The bankruptcy of Rolls-Royce shocked the nation.
('Trauma' is a sloppy use of a technical term. 'Real precedent' is a cliché. The revised version is simpler and clearer to the reader.)

References and bibliographies

Exercise 70

A bibliography is a list of books giving details of their authorship, publishers, editions, etc. A bibliography can include other printed items; for example, papers published in learned journals.

Exercise 71

(a)   Clew, K. R., *The Kennet & Avon Canal* (David & Charles, 1968)

(b)   Wilkie, Thomas, *British Science and Politics since 1945* (Basil Blackwell, 1991)

(c)   Guy, Josephine M., *The British Avant-Garde* (Harvester Wheatsheaf, 1991)

Exercise 73

(a)   Lovell, Bernard, 'Into the cosmic depths', *Times Literary Supplement*, issue 4610 (9 August 1991), p. 7

(b)   (i)   Nicholls, D., 'Theories of acids and bases', *Chemistry Student*, vol. 1, no. 2 (1967), pp. 33–8

(ii)   Nicholls, D., 'Theories of acids and bases', reprinted in J. G. Start (ed.), *Modern Chemistry* (Penguin, 1970), pp. 191–204

Exercise 74

(a)   Solo, Robert A., *The Philosophy of Science and Economics* (Macmillan (NY), 1991)

(b)   Alexander, William, and Street, Arthur, *Metals in the Service of Man*, 3rd edn (Penguin, 1946)

(c)   Parsons, R., 'Electrolysis and simple cells', *Contemporary Physics*, vol. 10, no. 3 (1969), pp. 205–20

(d)   Al Hassan, Ahmad Y., and Hill, Donald R., *Islamic Technology: an Illustrated History* (Cambridge University Press, 1991)

Bibliography

Plain English has been prepared with the help of many books dealing with various aspects of writing plain English.

Below are listed some books you may find interesting and useful for your studentship and beyond.

Barrass, R., *Scientists Must Write* (Chapman and Hall, 1978)

Carey, G. V., *Mind the Stop* (Penguin, 1977)

Collinson, D. J., *Writing English* (Wildwood House, 1986)

Fowler, H. W., *Modern English Usage*, 2nd edn (Oxford University Press, 1990)

Gowers, E., *The Complete Plain Words*, 3rd edn, rev. S. Greenbaum and J. Whitcut (Penguin, 1987)

McKaskill, Stanley G., *A Dictionary of Good English*, rev. edn (Macmillan, 1982)

MHRA Style Book, 4th edn (Modern Humanities Research Association, 1991)

Miller, C. and Swift, K., *The Handbook of Non-Sexist Writing*, 2nd edn (The Women's Press, 1989)

Phythian, B. A., *English Grammar* (Hodder & Stoughton, 1981)

Roget, P. M., *Roget's Thesaurus*, rev. edn (Penguin, 1988)

Dictionaries

Allen, R. E. (ed.), *The Oxford Spelling Dictionary* (Oxford University Press, 1986; paperback 1990)

Chambers English Dictionary, rev. edn (Chambers/Cambridge University Press, 1990)

Collocott, T. C. and Dobson, A. B. (eds), *Chambers Science and Technology Dictionary* (W. & R. Chambers, 1988)

Dictionary of Computing, 3rd edn (Oxford University Press, 1990)

Harraps Dictionary of Science and Technology (Harraps, 1991)

Webster's Third International Dictionary (Merriam-Webster, 1990)

121